KEN HOM
CHINESE
RECIPES

BOOKS FOR REAL COOKS

PAVILION

Pavilion Books for Real Cooks

Published in Great Britain in 1994 by
PAVILION BOOKS LIMITED
26 Upper Ground, London SE1 9PD

Recipes and Text © Taurom, Inc. 1994

Recipes originally published by Pavilion in
The Taste of China

Design by Write Image
Jacket photograph © Gus Filgate

A CIP catalogue record for this book is available from
the British Library

ISBN 1 85793 388 5

Printed and bound by WBC Printers, UK

2   4   6   8   10   9   7   5   3   1

This book may be ordered by post direct from the
publisher. Please contact the Marketing Department.
But try your bookshop first.

CONTENTS

FOREWORD

From Beijing (Peking) in the very cold north to Guangzhou (Canton) in the hot subtropical south, China's cuisine reflects the country's long history and its vast geographic and climatic variations. The dominant Asian power for thousands of years, China drew to herself the riches of the surrounding realms, including their culinary resources. Reciprocally, Chinese influences radiated out: there is simply no Asian cuisine that does not show traces of the Chinese kitchen.

The Chinese approach to food is that all of nature's offerings and culture's creations are eligible for the Chinese table. All that matters are high standards of taste, texture, aroma, colour, and even nutritional content, in harmonious combination.

I observed this amalgamation of styles and this receptivity to new ingredients as a child working in my uncle's restaurant in America. My family is of Cantonese (Guangdong) origin and is naturally partial to that region's cuisine. The restaurant, using ingredients available locally, prepared and served authentic Chinese food. Moreover, my uncle's chefs were from many regions in China, and I learned at an early age the diversity of Chinese culinary techniques and styles. These regional variations are customarily grouped into four broad categories.

The Southern School is most easily identified as Cantonese cuisine, which is perhaps the style most familiar to Westerners simply because so many overseas Chinese were originally from that region. The culinary style they carried with them emphasizes freshness of ingredients and quick-cooking to preserve the natural qualities of foods; stir-frying and steaming are the most popular cooking techniques. The famous dim sum – snacks and light lunches – demonstrate the best of the south's light and imaginative touch. Guangdong is one of the rice bowls of China, and rice is the staple of southern meals.

The Northern School encompasses the area bounded by the Great Wall and the Yangzi River, and includes the Shandong, Henan and Beijing (Peking) styles. This regional cuisine is most distinguishable because of its reliance on grains such as wheat, millet and corn instead of rice. Thus, breads, dumplings, noodles and pancakes are prominent and, because of the harsh winters, the Northern School specializes in dried, pickled and smoked meats and vegetables, and in the use of vegetables that store well – sweet potatoes, turnips, onions and cabbages.

The Eastern School radiates inland from the coast, especially from the area of Shanghai, China's largest city and greatest seaport. The area contains some of the most bountiful land in all of China, yielding rich crops of fruits and vegetables; rivers, lakes and the long seacoast provide a plentiful supply of fresh fish and seafood.

The Western School includes the isolated and exotic provinces of Sichuan and Hunan. The land here is abundant, rich in fruits and vegetables, pork, duck, chickens and river fish. The most distinguishing characteristic of this region's cuisine is its assertive flavouring and hot spices such as red chillis (dry and fresh), Sichuan peppercorns, ginger, spring onions and garlic.

With all this variation, Chinese cooking still clings to a few simple, shared themes, relying heavily on fresh and preserved vegetables, or a staple grain such as rice, or fish and seafood, almost excluding meat. Cooking techniques, whether fast or slow, preserve nutrients, flavours and textures. The famous yin and yang philosophy so respected in Chinese cuisine may be seen as no more than a reliance on certain combinations of foods and ingredients, prepared in certain ways, and sometimes reserved for certain situations. For example, some foods are always regarded as medicines or restoratives.

Typically a meal consists of a staple grain in any number of forms, and three or four separate dishes of vegetables and fish or meat, enhanced, but never obscured, by sauces and dips. Soups are served as a beverage throughout the meal. All of the dishes are set in the middle of the table for sharing among all diners. Eating is a communal experience shared by family and friends.

This book offers representative samples of authentic Chinese cuisine, with a glossary of the essential, authentic ingredients at the back. The recipes reflect the vastness of the country and its cultural diversity; yet within these regional variations is a cohesive, venerable tradition of devotion to food and its preparation. And don't be bound by any notion that Chinese food is somehow a separate part of your culinary experience: a Chinese-style salad in the summer, for example, or a warming soup in cold weather can start a meal of any sort. Chinese cuisine is remarkably adaptable to any ingredients, as long as they are the freshest.

Ken Hom
California,
December 1993

APPETIZERS

Leng Yacai

BEAN SPROUT SALAD

**SERVES 4 AS PART OF A
CHINESE MEAL, OR 2 AS A
SINGLE DISH**

1lb/ 450 g fresh bean
sprouts

3 tbsp white rice vinegar

1 ½ tbsp sugar

1 tsp salt

W hat we call "bean sprouts" come from the mung beans, which are grown in almost every part of China. They are a popular delicacy – crunchy, subtly flavored, and nutritious – as well as inexpensive. You rarely see them in the markets because they require proper refrigeration which is uncommon in China. Fragile, they must be eaten very soon after they sprout or they will lose their fresh, lovely taste. Some of the best I sampled were elegantly served at a Hangzhou restaurant; the recipe is below.

METHOD

Pluck the bean sprouts at both ends. Rinse them well in cold water and blanch them for 20 seconds in a large pot of boiling water. Remove the sprouts with a slotted spoon, and immediately plunge them in cold water. Drain thoroughly.

Combine the vinegar, sugar, and salt in a small bowl, mixing until the sugar and salt have dissolved. Toss the bean sprouts in the dressing and serve, or cover with plastic wrap and refrigerate for up to 2 hours.

Leng Donggua

WINTER MELON SALAD

W|inter melon has nourished Asians since earliest times. Today it's mainly used in soups, so this unusual salad made with slightly pickled winter melon was a delightful surprise for me when I first sampled it in Hangzhou. Juicy and slightly bland, winter melons are large but you can buy them by the slice in Chinese grocers'. Use watermelon if winter melon is unavailable.

METHOD

Remove the seeds and coarse fibres from the centre of the melon. With a sharp knife, cut away the peel and rinse well under cold water. Cut the melon into long shreds.

Sprinkle the shreds with the salt and allow them to sit in a colander set inside a bowl for 10 minutes. Rinse them in cold water, blot them dry, and toss with the sugar and vinegar. Refrigerate for 1 hour before serving.

SERVES 4 AS PART OF A CHINESE MEAL, OR 2 AS A SINGLE DISH

1 ½ lb/ 700 g fresh winter melon

1 tsp salt

1 tbsp sugar

1 tbsp white rice vinegar

Leng Oing Gua

COLD CUCUMBERS WITH GARLIC

**SERVES 4 AS PART OF A
CHINESE MEAL, OR 2 AS A
SINGLE DISH**

1 lb/ 450 g cucumbers

2 tsp salt

2 tsp sugar

1 tbsp white rice vinegar

1 ½ tbsp peanut oil

1 tbsp coarsely chopped
garlic

Recently in China, the loosening of state controls has encouraged a number of family-run private enterprises, among them new restaurants. It was at one such place in Shanghai that I enjoyed this delightful cold dish, a refreshing starter on a humid summer night. I have modified the recipe slightly, since I found the bits of raw garlic in the original version too strong. A quick browning of the garlic in the wok gives off a wonderful aroma.

METHOD

Slice the cucumbers in half lengthways and, using a spoon, remove any seeds. Cut the cucumber halves into 3 × ½ in/ 7.5 cm × 12 mm pieces.

Combine the cucumber pieces with salt and allow to sit in a colander set inside a bowl for 10 minutes. Rinse them in cold water, blot them dry and toss with the sugar and vinegar.

Heat a wok or large frying pan until hot and add the oil and garlic. Stir-fry for 15 seconds until it is lightly brown. Mix with the cucumbers and serve.

Leng Pan

TOMATO AND EGG SUMMER SALAD

This quick and easy salad consists of fresh tomatoes and two types of eggs, hard-boiled chicken eggs and preserved duck eggs, also known as thousand-year-old eggs. Buried in fine ash, salt, and lime for one hundred days, the eggs emerge with an aspic-like blackened jelly surrounding a greenish yolk, having been slow cooked by the action of the lime. Their distinctive, pungent flavor and aroma is reminiscent of strong cheese.

METHOD

Boil the fresh eggs for exactly 10 minutes. Remove them with a slotted spoon, immerse them immediately in cold water, and crack them lightly with the back of a spoon. Let them sit for at least 10 minutes in the cold water, changing the water two or three times. Gently peel the eggs. With a sharp knife, cut them in half.

Rinse the preserved eggs in cold water, peel them, and cut them in the same manner.

With a sharp knife, cut the tomatoes into thin slices. Arrange them in the middle of a large round platter. Sprinkle evenly with the sugar. Then alternately arrange a boiled egg half with a preserved egg half around the edge of the platter. Serve at once.

SERVES 4 AS PART OF A CHINESE MEAL, OR 2 AS A SINGLE DISH

2 fresh eggs

2 preserved (thousand-year-old) eggs

1 lb/ 450 g ripe tomatoes

1 ½ tbsp sugar

Yangru Bing
TOASTED GOAT CHEESE

**SERVES 4 AS PART OF A
CHINESE MEAL, OR 2 AS A
SINGLE DISH**

---

8 oz/ 225 g firm, mild
goat cheese or feta

Freshly ground black
pepper

C heese is a food rarely associated with Chinese cuisine. Although there are no taboos associated with milk and dairy products, they are generally not eaten by the Chinese, for historical, climatic, and other reasons. For instance, by age six, the Chinese – and the majority of the world's people – cease producing the enzyme lactase required for digesting milk and unprocessed dairy products. Processed milk products such as evaporated and sweetened condensed milk and mild cheeses are only now being introduced into some regions of China, though whole milk, yogurt, and especially goat cheeses have been popular for decades among the Muslims and other minority groups in the province of Yunnan, in the southwest. This firm, lightly toasted cheese is a speciality of that region.

METHOD

Cut the goat cheese into ¼ in/ 6 mm slices, then into 2 × 3 in/5 × 7.5 cm pieces.

Preheat the grill. Lay the goat cheese slices on a baking tray. Place it under the grill and cook until brown, about 5 minutes. Turn them over, brown the other side, sprinkle with the pepper and serve warm.

Ban Doufu

Tofu Salad

C hina is the place where soybeans were first cultivated over three thousand years ago. By the first millennium BC, the soybean was already enshrined as one of the five sacred grains, the others being millet, glutinous millet, wheat, and rice.

This recipe is a local speciality of Shanghai and involves no cooking. Extremely nutritious, but rather bland, soft and silky-smooth bean curd needs only a touch of taste and texture. Here the dried shrimp and preserved vegetables turn it into a truly delightful first course. Very fresh bean curd is essential. Serve this dish cold.

Method

Gently drain the bean curd and soak in several changes if cold water. Drain it again thoroughly and cut it into 1 in/ 25 mm cubes. Place the bean curd on a serving platter and refrigerate.

Soak the dried shrimp in warm water for 20 minutes and drain thoroughly. Finely chop the shrimp and place in a small bowl with the preserved vegetables and chili bean sauce. Arrange this mixture evenly over the bean curd and drizzle with the sesame oil. Garnish with the spring onions and serve at once.

Serves 4 as part of a Chinese meal, or 2 as a single dish

1 lb/ 450 g fresh soft bean curd

2 tbsp dried shrimp

2 tbsp Sichuan preserved vegetables, rinsed and finely chopped

1 tbsp chili bean sauce

1 ½ tbsp sesame oil

Garnish

1–2 chopped spring onions

Chun Juan

SPRING ROLLS

Makes 15 to 20 spring rolls

8 oz/ 225 g cabbage, finely chopped and blanched

4 oz/ 125 g minced pork

4 oz/ 125 g medium-sized uncooked prawns, peeled and finely chopped

1 oz/ 25 g dried black mushrooms, soaked, stems removed and finely chopped

3 tbsp dark soy sauce

1 tbsp rice wine or dry sherry

1 tbsp sesame oil

1 tsp salt

1 tsp freshly ground black pepper

1 egg, beaten and mixed with 1 tbsp water

1 package spring roll skins, thawed if frozen

1 ½ pints/ 850 ml peanut oil

These nutritious snacks, as their name suggests, symbolize and commemorate the coming of the spring season. They are among the traditional foods eaten in China on New Year's Eve, which, by the Chinese lunar calendar, marks the end of the winter season; such foods as spring rolls and dumplings are always at hand then for family and for visitors, although they are also enjoyed all year round.

The spring roll wrappers are thin and almost transparent, but they are firm enough to hold a substantial morsel of finely chopped meat, meat and vegetables, or just vegetables. In keeping with the Chinese tradition dictating that for the first two days of the new year no work, including housework, be done, they are especially appropriate because they can be made ahead but retain their flavor when frozen. In northern China, where the below-freezing days of February allow it, the prepared rolls are easily kept on trays outdoors until ready for cooking.

METHOD

In a medium-sized bowl, combine the cabbage, pork, prawns, mushrooms, soy sauce, rice wine or sherry, sesame oil, salt and pepper and mix thoroughly.

Combine the egg and water in a small bowl. Place about 4 tablespoons of cabbage filling on each spring roll skin and fold in each side and roll up tightly. Use the egg mixture to seal the edge.

Heat a wok or large frying pan until hot and add the oil. When the oil is quite hot, gently drop in as many spring rolls as will fit easily in one layer. Carefully fry them in batches until the spring rolls are golden brown on the outside and cooked inside, about 4 minutes. Adjust the heat as necessary. Remove the spring rolls with a slotted spoon and drain on kitchen paper. Serve them at once, while still hot and crispy.

Jiaozi-Guotie

BOILED AND PAN-FRIED MEAT DUMPLINGS

Makes about 36 dumplings

Dough skin

10 oz/ 275 g unbleached white flour

8–12 fl oz/ 225–350 ml very hot water

Filling

8 oz/ 225 g cabbage, finely chopped

4 oz/ 125 g minced pork

4 oz/ 125 g medium-sized uncooked prawns, peeled and finely chopped

1 oz/ 25 g black mushrooms, soaked, stems removed, and finely chopped

1 tbsp light soy sauce

1 tbsp dark soy sauce

1 tbsp rice wine or dry sherry

1 tbsp sesame oil

1 tsp salt

1 tsp freshly ground black pepper

I n northern China, wheat is the preferred grain, and dumplings, boiled or pan-fried, are a favorite food especially at New Year. Dumplings are made in Beijing restaurants and homes. Each family prides itself on its own version, its own savory stuffings. This particular recipe is from the Qu family in Beijing. In their small kitchen we shared views on food and cooking as we prepared the dumplings, a family activity involving several generations of helpers and guests like myself.

The family showed me the two basic ways of cooking them, boiling half for jiaozi and pan-frying the others for guotie, which acquire a crisp brown crust on one side. They are always eaten with a variety of communal dipping sauces. The uncooked dumplings freeze well.

METHOD

Place the flour in a large mixing bowl. Add the hot water in a steady stream, mixing all the while with a fork or chopsticks until most of the water has been incorporated. If the mixture seems dry, add more water. The dough should be moist but not sticky. Remove the dough from the bowl and knead it on a floured board until it is smooth, about 5 minutes. Return the dough to the bowl, cover with a damp cloth and let it rest.

In a medium-sized bowl, combine the cabbage, pork, prawns, mushrooms, soy sauces, rice wine or sherry, sesame oil, salt, and pepper and mix thoroughly. Set the mixture aside.

Knead the dough on a floured board, dusting with a little flour if it is sticky. Form the dough into a roll about 18 in/ 45.5 cm long and about 1 in/ 25 mm in diameter. Take a sharp knife and cut the roll into 4 equal lengths. Cut each length into 8 pieces to make 36 equal segments. Press each segment with the palm of your hand and then roll it into a 3 ½ in/ 9 cm round. Continue rolling out all the rounds, covering them with a damp cloth.

Pinch one side of the dough until you have four pleats along the side, and the dough is rounded and shell-like. Place 2 teaspoons of filling in the centre of each round, making sure it fills the hollow. You may add more filling if necessary. Then fold the dough over the filling, pinching the two sides together until you have a half-moon dumpling. Continue until you have filled all the rounds. The dumplings can be frozen at this point until ready to use.

To fry the dumplings, heat a wok or large frying pan until hot. Add the peanut oil, then add the dumplings, pleated edge up, in a single layer. They should be crowded together. Cook the dumplings over medium heat until they are lightly browned on the bottoms. Pour in the very hot water, cover tightly, and cook vigorously for 2 minutes. Turn the heat down to a simmer and continue to cook for another 8 to 10 minutes or until most of the water has evaporated. Uncover the pan and continue cooking until all the moisture has evaporated and the pan is sizzling again and the dumplings are golden brown and crisp on the bottoms. Remove to a serving platter and serve at once with the dipping sauces.

If you are boiling the dumplings, drop them into a large pot of salted, boiling water for 2 minutes. Remove from the heat and leave them in the water for about 15 minutes. Remove the dumplings with a slotted spoon and serve them the same way as the fried dumplings.

3 tbsp peanut oil, for the wok

8 fl oz/ 225 ml very hot water, for the wok

Dipping sauces

Chili bean sauce

White rice vinegar

Dark soy sauce

Zhima Haizhe

SESAME JELLYFISH

SERVES 4 AS PART OF A
CHINESE MEAL, OR 2 AS A
SINGLE DISH

8 oz/ 225 g prepared
shredded jellyfish

2 tsp light soy sauce

3 tbsp sesame oil

2 tsp white rice vinegar

2 tsp sugar

3 tbsp white sesame
seeds, toasted

S ea cucumbers, limpets, sea slugs, barnacles, sea snakes – all the creatures of fresh and salt water that are big enough to eat and not outright poisonous are welcomed in Chinese cooking. This includes jellyfish, always bought dried. It is a textured, fat-free, protein food that makes a refreshing and crunchy appetizer. Salty and mild-tasting by itself, marinated jellyfish takes on another dimension with the sesame flavors permeating the slightly salty jellyfish to produce a cooling treat. This is traditionally served by itself and is an easy dish to prepare because the jellyfish comes already partially soaked and shredded in a package. This dish will stay fresh for hours in the refrigerator.

METHOD

Rince the jellyfish well in cold running water and drain. Put it in a stainless steel bowl and cover with boiling water. Let the jellyfish sit in the water for about 15 minutes or until it is tender. Drain and continue to soak at least 6 times in several changes of cold water. Drain thoroughly and blot dry with kitchen paper and set aside.

Mix soy sauce, sesame oil, vinegar, and sugar in a small bowl. Toss the jellyfish well in this sauce and let it sit for at least 30 minutes. Just before serving, garnish with the sesame seeds.

MEAT

Bu Xue Yang Yan Tang

SOUP FOR THE BLOOD AND SKIN

**SERVES 4 AS PART OF A
CHINESE MEAL, OR 2 AS A
SINGLE DISH**

4 oz/ 125 g raw peanuts

2 dried tangerine or
orange peels

12 dried red jujube
dates

3 pints/ 1.7 litres water

4 slices fresh ginger root

2 ½ lb/ 1.1 kg shin of
beef

2 teaspoons salt

Chinese medicinal herbalists believe that this soup is a potent tonic for one's blood and the skin which is the mirror of inner health. The ingredients illustrate the ancient Chinese theory that beef, being naturally sweet and "warm", strengthens vital energies in the blood and nourishes the spleen and stomach. It holds that beef's powers are enhanced when peanuts are added to the soup.

The soup also includes red jujube dates. These have been used in China since early times as a tonic nutrient and a purifying food when combined with certain other ingredients. They are believed to build strength, improve circulation, and extend life. Moreover, since they are naturally sweet and contribute a honey flavor to the soup, they make this particular medicine go down very easily. While the peanuts give the soup its milky-white color, dried tangerine or orange peel adds a pleasant tart element.

METHOD

Grind the peanuts coarsely in a blender or food processor and set aside. Soak the tangerine or orange peels in hot water for 20 minutes or until they are soft and drain. Soak the red jujube dates in warm water for 20 minutes, drain and set aside.

Bring the water to a boil in a large pot. Add the ground peanuts, tangerine or orange peels, ginger and dates. Add the beef and bring back to a boil, skimming the surface continually. Lower the heat to a simmer, cover and cook for 3 hours or until the beef is tender. Add the salt to taste.

Gan Bian Niurou

CRISP BEEF IN CHILI SAUCE

he Han Chinese eat very little beef, preferring pork, due to their history, method of farming, and philosophy. Muslim Chinese, on the other hand, don't eat pork and quite enjoy beef dishes. This version from a Muslim restaurant in southwest China is one of the tastiest I have ever had. The beef is first coated in a light batter, fried twice for extra crispness, and then tossed in a clear chili sauce that is at once sweet and spicy.

METHOD

Place the meat in the freezer for about 20 minutes, or until it is firm to the touch. Cut it into slices against the grain, then finely shred the slices. Combine the meat with the marinade and mix very well.

Soak the dried chilies in warm water. When they are soft and pliable, cut them in half.

Heat a wok or frying pan until it is hot. Add the peanut oil and when it is very hot and almost smoking, deep-fry the beef in two batches. Remove with a slotted spoon and drain the meat in a colander.

Heat a small saucepan and when it is hot, add the 1 ½ tbsp oil, garlic and chilies and stir-fry for 20 seconds. Then add the rest of the sauce ingredients and simmer for 2 minutes. Keep warm.

Reheat the oil in the wok until it is very hot. Deep-fry the beef again until it is very crisp, about 1 minute. Remove the beef with a slotted spoon, drain on kitchen paper and place on a warm plaster. Gently toss the beef with the sauce and serve immediately.

SERVES 4 AS PART OF A CHINESE MEAL, OR 2 AS A SINGLE DISH

1 lb/ 450 g beef steak

Marinade

1 tbsp light soy sauce

2 tsp rice wine

1 tsp sesame oil

½ tsp salt

3 tbsp cornflour

1 tbsp plain flour

16 fl oz/ 450 ml peanut oil

Sauce

5 dried chilies, halved

1 ½ tbsp peanut oil

3 tbsp finely sliced garlic

1 tsp salt

3 tbsp sugar

½ cup water

1 tsp cornflour mixed with 1 tsp water

Xiao Long Yan Rou

LAMB STEAMED WITH SPICE-FLAVORED CORNMEAL

SERVES 4 AS PART OF A CHINESE MEAL, OR 2 AS A SINGLE DISH

2 ½ oz/ 60 g yellow cornmeal

2 tsp five-spice powder

2 tsp ground roasted Sichuan peppercorns

1 tsp salt

1 lb/ 450 g lean lamb (fillet or leg)

3 tbsp finely chopped spring onions

2 tsp finely chopped garlic

2 tsp finely chopped peeled fresh ginger root

1 tbsp rice wine or dry sherry

1 tbsp light soy sauce

2 tsp sesame oil

In the original version of this northern Chinese recipe, the tender goat meat is coated with spiced cornmeal and gently steamed, then served in a bamboo steamer lined with linen cloth. I have used lamb in place of the rather more robust goat meat. The preparation is surprisingly easy.

METHOD

In a medium-sized bowl, combine the cornmeal, five-spice powder, ground Sichuan peppercorns and salt. Mix well and set aside.

Cut the lamb into thin strips, about ¼ in/ 6 mm thick by 3 in/ 7.5 cm long. In a large bowl, combine the lamb with the onions, garlic, ginger, rice wine or sherry, soy sauce, and sesame oil.

Lay the lamb in a large baking tray and toss with the cornmeal mixture to coat evenly. Arrange the lamb on a plate.

Set up a steamer or put a rack into a wok or deep pan. Fill the steamer with about 2 in/ 5 cm of hot water. Bring the water to a simmer. Put the plate with the lamb into the steamer or onto the rack. Cover the steamer tightly and gently steam over medium heat for 30 minutes. Replenish the water in the steamer from time to time as needed.

Serve at once.

Hongshao Yangrou

BRAISED LAMB OR GOAT CASSEROLE

**SERVES 6, OR 3 AS A
SINGLE DISH**

A lthough goat dishes may be found in many places, most Chinese find goat not to their taste. It is primarily eaten in the western regions of China, probably reflecting the Muslim influence there. Here is a recipe from the western province of Yunnan in which goat, or equally lamb, is braised in a casserole with an array of spices and other seasonings. The casserole makes a hearty meal in itself, but it can also serve as part of a larger meal. Since the dish reheats well, you could make it well ahead of time to freeze.

METHOD

Cut the meat into 2 in/ 5 cm dice. Remove the rind and blanch the meat in a large pot of boiling water for 5 minutes. Remove the meat and discard the water.

In a large pot or casserole, add the blanched meat and all the ingredients, adding more water as necessary so that all the meat is covered with liquid. Season with salt and freshly ground pepper. Bring the mixture to a boil, skim off any fat or foam from the surface, and turn the heat down as low as possible. Cover and braise for 2 hours or until the meat is very tender. Skim off any surface fat and serve.

3 lb/ 1.4 kg boneless goat or lamb shoulder

4 spring onions

4 slices peeled fresh ginger root

3 tbsp fermented bean curd

4 tbsp rice wine or dry sherry

3 tbsp light soy sauce

2 tbsp dark soy sauce

4 whole star anise

3 tbsp sugar

tbsp whole Sichuan peppercorns, roasted

2 cinnamon sticks

3 tbsp hoisin sauce

12 fl oz/ 350 ml chicken stock

3 ½–4 pints/ 900 ml–1 litre of water, or more

salt and pepper

Yangrou Xiangcai

STIR-FRIED LAMB OR GOAT WITH FRESH CORIANDER

SERVES 4 AS PART OF A CHINESE MEAL, OR 2 AS A SINGLE DISH

1 lb/ 450 g lean goat fillets, or lamb fillets, boneless loin or steaks

Marinade

2 tsp dark soy sauce

2 tsp rice wine or dry sherry

1 tsp sesame oil

½ tsp salt

½ tsp freshly ground black pepper

2 tsp cornflour

4 oz fresh mild chilies

2 tbsp peanut oil

handful of fresh coriander, washed

S outhwest China is mountainous but blessed with a wonderfully moderate climate. It is one of the most interesting and exotic regions of China, being populated by more than twenty-four different ethnic groups. The province's large Muslim population means that beef and mutton as well as goat are readily available, though pork is as popular there among other groups as it is in the rest of the country.

I had a fabulous dining experience in a hotel restaurant in Kunming (Yunnan): "the goat multi-dish banquet". It usually averages forty dishes, but the dish below was one in fifty-four! In it the strong assertive flavor of goat meat is tamed by seasonings such as fresh coriander; lamb is a perfectly good substitute.

METHOD

Cut the lamb into thin slices and combine it in a small bowl with the soy sauce, rice wine or sherry, sesame oil, pepper, and cornflour. Let the meat marinate for 30 minutes.

Seed and cut the chilies into thin slices.

Heat a wok or large frying pan until hot. Add the oil and when it smokes add the meat, stir-frying for 2 minutes or until it is browned. Remove with a slotted spoon.

Add the chilies and stir-fry for 2 to 3 minutes. Put in the fresh coriander and stir-fry another 2 minutes. Return the meat to the wok, give a couple of good stirs, and serve immediately.

Yan Jian Rou

STIR-FRIED CHILI PORK

S ichuan food is hot, spicy and sensual, and the chili is one of the mainstays of that region's cuisine. Unlike in the West, the Chinese do not offer chilies in oil or a paste at the table to augment tastes. Instead they season a dish before it arrives. Fragrant, roasted Sichuan peppercorns combined with freshly crushed dried chilies ensure some fire to the dish, though not all chilies used are hot. In this recipe mild chilies are combined with thinly sliced pork to create a nutritious dish which is colorful, fragrant and flavorful.

METHOD

Cut the pork into 3 in/ 7.5 cm thin slices and combine with the soy sauce, 1 tablespoon rice wine, salt and sesame oil.

Cut the chilies in half lengthwise and seed them.

Heat a wok or large frying pan until hot. Add the 1 ½ tablespoons of peanut oil and the pork and stir-fry for 1 minute. Remove the pork with a slotted spoon.

Reheat the wok or frying pan. Add the remaining oil. When it is very hot, add the fresh chilies, garlic, chili powder, and peppercorns and stir-fry for 30 seconds. Then add the water, 1 tablespoon rice wine or sherry, soy sauce, and sugar and cook for another 30 seconds. Return the meat to the mixture and heat through. Stir well, turn onto a platter, and serve.

SERVES 4 AS PART OF A CHINESE MEAL, OR 2 AS A SINGLE DISH

1 lb/ 450 g lean pork

1 tbsp light soy sauce

2 tbsp rice wine or dry sherry

pinch of salt

2 tsp sesame oil

8 oz/ 225 g fresh mild chilies

3 tbsp peanut oil

3 tbsp finely chopped garlic

1 tsp ground red chili powder

1 tsp Sichuan peppercorns, roasted and crushed

3 tbsp water

1 tbsp light soy sauce

2 tsp sugar

Huang Gua Chao Roupian

CUCUMBERS STIR-FRIED WITH PORK

**SERVES 4 AS PART OF A
CHINESE MEAL, OR 2 AS A
SINGLE DISH**

8 oz/ 225 g lean
boneless pork

2 tsp light soy sauce

1 tsp dark soy sauce

1 tsp rice wine or dry
sherry

1 tsp sesame oil

½ tsp cornflour

1 lb/ 450 g cucumbers

1 ½ tbsp peanut oil

1 tbsp chili bean sauce

2 tsp finely chopped
garlic

1 tsp roasted ground
Sichuan peppercorns

½ tsp chili flakes or chili
powder

½ tsp salt

2 tsp light soy sauce

2 tsp rice wine or dry
sherry

2 tsp white rice vinegar

1 tsp sugar

ellow cucumbers, really large, heavy, and firm melons, have a crisp, cool flesh and mild taste. They are often stir-fried or used in soup, where they give a distinctive flavor to the broth. If pickled, the cucumber is often eaten unpeeled. Being a "cooling" food, it is considered beneficial to the body during hot weather. They can be found at Asian markets; if unavailable, use the more familiar green cucumbers which come a close approximation in taste.

METHOD

Cut the pork into thin slices, about ⅛ in/ 3 mm thick by 3 in/ 7.5 cm long. In a medium-sized bowl, combine the pork with soy sauces, rice wine or sherry, sesame oil and cornflour and set aside.

Peel the cucumbers, split them in half lengthwise and with a spoon, scoop out the seeds, then finely slice the flesh crosswise.

Heat a wok or large frying pan until hot. Add the oil, then chili bean sauce, garlic, Sichuan peppercorns, chili flakes and salt and stir-fry for 10 seconds. Then add the pork, and continue to stir-fry for 1 minute. Put in the cucumbers and stir-fry for 1 minute. Pour in the soy sauce, rice wine or sherry, vinegar, and sugar. Continue to stir-fry for 2 minutes or until all the liquid has evaporated. Serve at once.

C h a o D o u y a

STIR-FRIED SOYBEAN SPROUTS
WITH PORK

S oybean sprouts are a nutritious and eco-
nomical food, used in China as an "instant
vegetable". Similar to mung bean sprouts but
longer and with a large yellow bean seed attached,
soybean sprouts add crunchiness and a nut-like
flavor to recipes. They are available in Chinese
markets, though the more widely available mung
bean sprouts are an acceptable substitute.

This simple stir-fry of marinated pork bits is
enhanced by shrimp paste, a typical south Chinese
condiment; its strong odor is rendered more pleasant by cooking.

METHOD
Chop the pork into small coarse bits. In a small
bowl, combine it with the rice wine or sherry, soy
sauce, sesame oil and cornflour. Wash the sprouts
in cold running water, picking out any wilted
pieces of darkened sprouts. Drain well.

Heat a wok or large fying pan until hot. Add
2 tablespoons of oil and the ginger pieces. When
the ginger has browned, remove it with a slotted
spoon. Put in the pork and stir-fry for 2 minutes.
Remove the pork with a slotted spoon.

Reheat the wok or pan and add the remaining
oil. When it is very hot, add the shrimp paste and
stir-fry it for 10 seconds. Then add the sprouts
and soy sauce. Continue to stir-fry for 4 minutes.
Return the pork to the wok and mix very well with
the sauce, continuously stir-frying for another
minute. Give the mixture several good stirs, turn
onto a platter and serve.

**SERVES 4 AS PART OF A
CHINESE MEAL, OR 2 AS A
SINGLE DISH**

8 oz/ 225 g lean pork

1 tsp rice wine or dry
sherry

1 tsp light soy sauce

½ tsp sesame oil

½ tsp cornflour

1 ½ lb/ 700 g soybean
sprouts or mung bean
sprouts

2 tbsp peanut oil

2 slices peeled fresh
ginger root, crushed

1 tbsp peanut oil

1 tsp shrimp paste

2 tsp light soy sauce

Chao Nai

STIR-FRIED MILK

**SERVES 4 AS PART OF A
CHINESE MEAL, OR 2 AS A
SINGLE DISH**

16 fl oz/ 450 ml milk

1 tsp salt

½ tsp freshly ground
white pepper

4 tbsp cornflour

1 tbsp peanut oil, for the
baking pan

1 ½ tbsp peanut oil

1 tsp salt

8 oz/ 225 g Chinese
barbecue pork or mild
ham, coarsely chopped

4 oz/ 100 g medium-
sized uncooked prawns
unpeeled (but without
heads) or 12–13 oz/
350–375 g peeled
uncooked prawns,
coarsely chopped

4 oz/ 100 g pine nuts

I have sampled many versions of this tasty dish in Hong Kong and in the southern province of Guangdong. This memorable version was served at a Shunde restaurant. The "milk" is really a thick custard, stir-fried with prawns, barbecued Chinese pork, and pine nuts, a perfect combination of taste and textures. I was told by the residents of the town that cows are abundant in the area and that milk-based dishes have been part of the local cuisine for a long time. In a country with almost no dairy products, Cantonese milk dishes date from the Portuguese influence of over three hundred years ago. Exposed to the European tradition, the Cantonese created exceptionally flavorful dishes in which they cook the milk first to make it more digestible.

METHOD

Combine the milk, salt, pepper, and cornflour in a medium-sized saucepan and mix until smooth. Then simmer the mixture over low heat for 8 minutes or until it has thickened to a consistency of soft scrambled eggs. Oil a baking pan, pour in the cooked milk mixture, and allow it to cool thoroughly. Cover with plastic wrap and refrigerate. This can be done the day before.

Heat a wok or large frying pan until hot and add the oil and salt. Then add the barbecue pork or ham and prawns, and stir-fry the mixture for 1 minute. Add the milk mixture and pine nuts, and stir-fry for 3 minutes or until the entire dish is heated through. Serve at once.

Shen Tui

"FANTASY PORK"

I was very encouraged when I first tasted this dish in a restaurant in Yunnan, Kunming, because it catered to my ideal of Chinese cooking with its straightforward, careful preparation and attention to a balance of flavors. It was properly braised with just the right seasonings to give the meat a robust but not overpowering fragrance. The rich wine sauce and subtle sweetness of the other ingredients combined beautifully with the taste of pork.

This dish is easy to prepare, and can be made ahead of time. It reheats well and is also very good served cold – perfect for a dinner party.

METHOD

Dry the ham thoroughly with kitchen paper.

Cut the spring onions into 3 in/ 7.5 cm segments.

Choose a heavy casserole pot, large enough to hold the ham comfortably. Heat the pot and then add the oil, ginger, garlic, and onions, and stir-fry in the pot for 2 minutes. Push the aromatics to the side and brown the ham on each side until it has some color, 10 to 15 minutes. Pour off the oil.

Add all the braising liquid ingredients to the pot and bring the mixture to a boil. Turn the heat down to a simmer, cover tightly, and cook for about 4 ½ hours, turning the ham from time to time. When the ham is tender, remove it gently with a large spatula. The meat should be literally falling apart. Place it on a serving platter.

Strain the sauce, skim off any surface fat, and reduce the liquid until it is slightly thick. Pour this over the ham and serve.

SERVES 8 TO 10 AS PART OF A CHINESE MEAL, OR 4 TO 6 AS A SINGLE DISH

fresh ham, about 5 lb/ 2.3 kg

8 spring onions

3 tbsp peanut oil

8 slices fresh ginger root

4 garlic cloves peeled and crushed

Braising liquid

2 pints/ 1.1 litres hot water

8 fl oz/ 225 ml dark soy sauce

8 fl oz/ 225 ml rice wine or dry sherry

3 tbsp whole roasted Sichuan peppercorns

6 tbsp rock or ordinary sugar

4 star anise

2 cinnamon sticks or bark

2 tsp five-spice powder

1 tsp salt

Dong Po Rou

TUNG PO PORK

**SERVES 6 AS PART OF A
CHINESE MEAL, OR 3 AS A
SINGLE DISH**

2-2 ½ lb/ 900 g-1.1 kg
fresh bacon
———
3 tbsp peanut oil
———
6 spring onions
———
6 fresh ginger root slices
———
4 oz/ 125 g rock sugar,
crushed, or 4 tbsp sugar
———
4 fl oz/ 125 ml dark soy
sauce
———
2 tbsp light soy sauce
———
4 fl oz/ 125 ml rice wine
or dry sherry
———
4 fl oz/ 125 ml water

T his delicious dish is named for Su Dongpo, a famous poet, statesman and gourmet of the Song Dynasty, whose combination of talents is not uncommon in Chinese history. I certainly admire him for his many culinary skills, and especially for inventing this savory dish. Dong Po pork is a house speciality in several restaurants in Hangzhou where Su Dongpo was a governor of the city. Gentle, long, slow simmering renders the meat into a melting, buttery, tender gastronomic experience. The cut used is pork belly, referred to as "five-flowered" pork in Chinese. There seems to be many versions of this popular dish in restaurants throughout China, but my favorite is this one in which the skin is first browned; in addition, simmering the pork in a whole piece keeps the meat moist. Although this preparation is time-consuming the dish is relatively simple, and it reheats well. It is wonderful served with plain rice and stir-fried vegetables.

METHOD

Blanch the fresh bacon in a pot of boiling water for 10 minutes. Remove with a slotted spoon and blot thoroughly dry with kitchen paper.

Heat a wok or large frying pan until hot. Add the oil, turn down the heat, add the fresh bacon, skin side down. Slowly brown the skin until it is golden and crispy. This should take about 10 to 15 minutes. Remove the meat and wipe off any excess fat with kitchen paper.

Cut the onions into 3 in/ 7.5 cm pieces. In a large heavy casserole pot, combine the onions, ginger, rock sugar, the soy sauces, rice wine or sherry, water and meat together. Bring the mixture to a simmer, cover tightly, and cook slowly over low heat for 3 hours or until the pork is very tender and much of the fat is rendered.

Drain off the liquid, remove the onions and ginger. Skim off any surface fat. Cut the pork into thin slices, arrange on a platter, pour the sauce over and serve.

Chengdu Huntun

CHENGDU WONTONS

SERVES 4, OR 2 AS A SINGLE DISH

1 package wonton skins (about 30 to 35 skins)

Filling

12 oz/ 350 g minced pork

1 egg, beaten

1 tbsp sesame oil

2 tsp salt

½ tsp freshly ground black pepper

1 tbsp garlic

4 tbsp spring onions

3 tbsp dark soy sauce

1 tbsp sugar

1 tbsp chili oil

2 tsp Chinese black vinegar

¼ tsp freshly ground black pepper

Garnish

1 tbsp Sichuan peppercorns, roasted and ground

Huntuns are simply dumplings, well-known in the West mostly by their Cantonese name, wontons. The skins (usually made from wheat) are filled with meat or fish or vegetables in a seasoned sauce. They are in the *xiao chi* ("small eats") repertory but are also found as part of complete menus. The filling and sauce will vary with the region and the season. I discovered this version at a delightful shop in Chengdu, Sichuan, that specializes in dumplings. The authentic taste requires these wontons to be hot and spicy, but you may tone this down a bit by reducing the amount of chili oil.

METHOD

Combine the pork, egg, sesame oil, salt and pepper in a large bowl and mix well. Then, using a teaspoon, put a small amount of the filling in the center of each wonton skin. Bring up two sides, dampen the edges with a little water, and pinch them together to seal. Continue until you have used up all the filling or wonton skins.

Finely chop the garlic and spring onions. In a large serving bowl, combine them with the soy sauce, sugar, chili oil, vinegar and pepper. Stir to mix well.

Bring a large pot of water to the boil. Put in the wontons and simmer for 4 minutes. Remove them with a slotted spoon to the serving bowl. Mix gently with the sauce, garnish with peppercorns, and serve at once.

Liang Ban Rou
___

TWICE-COOKED PORK

This dish is often served in Sichuan-style restaurants in the West. Rarely is it served properly because the authentic cut of meat, namely pork belly, is fatty. Westerners usually avoid it, thinking it's unpalatable. This is unfortunate because pork belly, properly prepared, is meltingly tender and rich, and without a trace of fat.

To achieve this, pork belly requires a good bit of cooking, traditionally simmered in water with spring onions and ginger in enormous woks for what seems like hours. When removed, the meat is allowed to cool and sliced thinly, blanched again, and served with a homemade hot chili sauce. I have changed the recipe slightly by stir-frying the pork instead of blanching it a second time. Because the dish reheats so well, much of the work can be done ahead of time.

METHOD

Add to a pot of boiling water, the pork belly, whole onions, ginger and salt. Cover tightly and simmer for 1½ hours. Remove the meat with a slotted spoon and drain well. Discard the cooking liquid. When the pork belly has cooled thoroughly, cut it into thin ¼ in/ 6 mm pieces.

Cut the other spring onions into 3 in/ 7.5 cm pieces. Heat a wok or large frying pan until hot. Add the oil and the pork slices and stir-fry for 10 minutes. Drain off any excess oil. Add the garlic and ginger and stir-fry for 10 seconds. Add the scallions and continue to stir-fry for 3 minutes. Then add the rest of the ingredients and stir-fry for another 3 minutes, mixing well. Serve at once.

SERVES 6 AS PART OF A CHINESE MEAL, OR 3 AS A SINGLE DISH

2-2 ½ lb/ 900 g-1.1 kg fresh bacon or pork belly
___
6 whole spring onions
___
6 slices peeled fresh ginger root
___
1 tbsp salt
___
6 spring onions
___
3 tbsp peanut oil
___
2 tbsp finely chopped garlic
___
1 tbsp finely chopped peeled fresh ginger root
___
1 ½ tbsp chili bean sauce
___
1 tbsp rice wine or dry sherry
___
1 tbsp light soy sauce
___
2 tsp sugar
___
1 tsp salt
___

Gulao Rou

SWEET AND SOUR PORK MADE WITH FRUIT JUICE

SERVES 4 AS PART OF A
CHINESE MEAL, OR 2 AS A
SINGLE DISH

———

1 ½ lb/ 700 g boneless
pork neck on the fatty
side

———

½ tsp salt

———

1 tbsp light soy sauce

———

2 tsp rice wine or dry
sherry

———

2 tsp sesame oil

———

1 egg, beaten

———

1 tbsp cornflour

———

2 tbsp peanut oil

———

8 oz/ 225 g whole
shallots, peeled

———

2 tbsp sugar

———

3 tbsp Chinese red
vinegar

———

10 fl oz/ 275 ml freshly
squeezed orange juice

———

1 tsp cornflour mixed
with 2 tsp water

———

Salt and freshly ground
pepper to taste

———

This dish is often on menus in mediocre Chinese restaurants in the West where it invariably appears as a sweet, gluey, reddish concoction. This version, however, captures the virtues of the classic dish "Gulao Pork". In China, gulao means venerable. A sour taste is obtained from such fruits as plums, oranges and berries, then combined with sweetened vinegar and other seasonings. Here I use fresh orange juice along with sugar and vinegar. The "sweets" and "sours" combine and penetrate the meat, while the shallots provide a rich and fragrant background.

METHOD

Cut the pork into 2 in/ 50 cm chunks and combine with the salt, soy sauce, rice wine or sherry, sesame oil, egg and the tablespoon of cornflour. Mix well and let the mixture sit for about 30 minutes.

In a small saucepan, heat the oil and add the shallots and sugar. Cook over low heat until the sauce becomes a light caramel color, about 2 minutes. Pour in the vinegar and orange juice and simmer for 4 minutes. Gently beat in the cornflour mixture, and when the sauce thickens, season to taste with salt and pepper. Set the sauce aside and keep warm.

Combine the flour and 3 oz/ 75 g cornflour together in a large paper bag. Add the marinated pork pieces, close the bag, and toss well to coat each piece of pork. Shake off the excess flour.

Heat a wok or large frying pan until hot. Add the oil and a few pork pieces and deep-fry until cooked through, about 4 minutes. You will have to do this in several batches. Remove the pork with a slotted spoon and drain on kitchen paper.

Drain off all the oil from the wok or pan, wipe it clean, and reheat the sauce. Return the fried pork pieces to the wok and stir to coat well with the sauce. Serve at once.

3 oz/ 75 g unbleached plain flour

3 oz/ 75 g cornflour

16 fl oz/ 450 ml peanut oil

Chao Sansi

THREE-SHREDDED DISH

SERVES 4 TO 6 AS PART OF A CHINESE MEAL, OR 2 TO 4 AS A SINGLE DISH

8 oz/ 225 g fresh pork liver

2 tsp light soy sauce

1 tsp rice wine or dry sherry

Pinch of salt and pepper

1 tsp cornflour

1 tsp sesame oil

8 oz/ 225 g boneless lean pork

1 tsp light soy sauce

1 tsp rice wine or dry sherry

Pinch of salt and pepper

1 tsp cornflour

1 tsp sesame oil

8 oz/ 225 g cooked boneless duck or chicken

4 eggs

1 tbsp cornflour mixed with 1 tbsp water

½ tsp salt

Exceptionally delicious, this recipe is a clear example of great Cantonese style in its contrasts of flavor, texture and style. I savored it at a small Shunde restaurant specializing in local dishes.

"Three-shredded" refers to the roast duck, pork and pork liver which are stir-fried in a savory sauce. Then they are placed on a bed of crisp, deep-fried egg shreds.

METHOD

Cut the liver lengthwise into 2 in/ 5 cm wide strips, then cut them crosswise into thin slices. Blanch them in boiling water for 40 seconds, remove with a slotted spoon, and plunge them immediately into cold water. Drain thoroughly and blot dry with kitchen paper. Combine the liver with the soy sauce, rice wine or sherry, salt, pepper, cornflour and 1 teaspoon sesame oil and set aside.

Cut the pork into thin slices in the same manner as the pork liver, and combine it with the soy sauce, rice wine or sherry, salt, pepper, cornflour and 1 teaspoon sesame oil.

Cut the cooked duck or chicken into slices the same size as the pork.

Beat the eggs in a small bowl and combine with the cornflour mixture, salt, and sesame oil. Heat a wok or large frying pan until hot and add the peanut oil. When the oil becomes hot, pour a small amount of the egg mixture into a strainer. When the egg drips through, rotate the strainer around the top of the wok to make a single layer of lace-like batter that covers the top of the oil.

Deep-fry the egg shreds in batches until they turn a golden brown, about 15 seconds. Remove the shreds with a slotted spoon and drain them on kitchen paper. Arrange on a platter and keep them warm in a low oven.

Drain off all but 2 tablespoons of oil and reheat the wok or pan. When it is hot, add the garlic, ginger, and onions and stir-fry for 30 seconds. Then add the pork liver and pork. Continue to stir-fry for 3 minutes. Then add the cooked duck or chicken, stock and soy sauces. Continue to stir-fry for 3 minutes. Thicken the sauce with the cornflour mixture, stir in the sesame oil, and give the mixture two final stirs. Serve this on top of the shredded fried egg.

1 tsp sesame oil

8 fl oz/ 450 ml peanut oil

1 ½ tbsp finely chopped garlic

2 tsp finely chopped ginger

4 tbsp finely chopped spring onions

4 fl oz/ 125 ml chicken stock

1 tbsp light soy sauce

2 tsp dark soy sauce

2 tsp cornflour mixed with 1 tbsp water

2 tsp sesame oil

Jiaoyan Pai Gu

SALT AND PEPPER SPARERIBS

**SERVES 4 AS PART OF A
CHINESE MEAL, OR 2 AS A
SINGLE DISH**

1 lb/ 450 g boneless
meaty spareribs or pork
shoulder

2 tsp light soy sauce

2 tsp rice wine or dry
sherry

1 tsp salt

1 tsp sesame oil

2 tsp cornflour

12 fl oz/ 350 ml peanut
oil

2 tbsp finely chopped
garlic

1 tsp salt

2 tsp roasted ground
Sichuan peppercorns

1 tsp five-spice powder

½ tsp chili powder

S hanghai chefs especially know how to coax out all of pork's best qualities. Here it is marinated, fried, and then stir-fried in a savory mixture of spices. I have modified this particular restaurant's recipe for convenience but without detracting from its excellent taste. And I have used boneless spareribs.

METHOD

Cut the pork into 1 in/ 25 mm cubes and combine it with the soy sauce, rice wine or sherry, salt, sesame oil and cornflour. Set aside for 15 minutes.

Heat a wok or large frying pan until hot. Add the oil, and when it is medium hot, deep-fry the pork until it is golden and crisp about 10 minutes. Remove the pork with a slotted spoon and drain off all but 2 tablespoons of the oil. Reheat the wok or pan and when it is hot, add the garlic and stir-fry for 10 seconds. Then add the salt, peppercorns, five-spice powder and chili powder and stir-fry for another 10 seconds. Return the fried pork to the wok or pan and continue to stir-fry over medium heat for about 3 minutes. Serve at once.

Zha Li Rou

FRIED STEWED COUNTRY SPARERIBS

One of the most cultured periods of Chinese history, and of Chinese cuisine, was that of the Southern Song Dynasty (1126–1279 AD). The Imperial Court gave banquets with hundreds of dishes. Among them were delights such as hearty spareribs, marinated with honey, stewed, and finally deep-fried. I very much enjoyed a re-creation of this dish in a Hangzhou restaurant; it offers a glimpse into the gastronomic delights of the Song court.

METHOD

In a large pot of boiling water, blanch the spareribs for 5 minutes. Drain thoroughly.

Rub the spareribs with the marinade and let sit for 30 minutes at room temperature.

In a medium-size clay pot or casserole, combine the chicken stock with the marinated spareribs. Bring the mixture to a simmer, cover, and cook for 15 minutes. Remove the spareribs with a slotted spoon. Reduce the liquid in the pot for 15 minutes over high heat or until it is slightly thick and syrupy. Return the spareribs to the pot and coat thoroughly with the mixture. Remove and allow the spareribs to dry, about 30 minutes to 1 hour.

Heat a wok or large skillet until it is hot. Add the oil and when it is medium hot, deep-fry the spareribs until they are crisp and golden. Drain on paper towels and serve at once.

SERVES 4 AS PART OF A CHINESE MEAL, OR 2 AS A SINGLE DISH

1 ½ lb/ 700 g meaty (country style) pork spareribs

Marinade

1 tbsp honey

1 ½ tbsp rice wine or dry sherry

2 tbsp light soy sauce

1 tbsp Chinese black rice vinegar

1 tbsp sugar

2 tsp ground roasted Sichuan peppercorns

1 tsp salt

12 fl oz/ 350 ml chicken stock

16 fl oz/ 450 ml peanut oil

Zhu Jiao Jiang Cu

PICKLED PIG'S TROTTERS AND GINGER

SERVES 4 TO 6 AS
APPETIZERS

3 lb/ 1.4 kg pig's
trotters, preferably from
the hind legs

1 ½ lb/ 850 ml Chinese
red or black rice vinegar

6 slices fresh ginger root

6 tbsp sugar

I can remember living in Chicago when my mother's friends gathered in our living room to celebrate the birth of a child. The food for such a party always included boiled red-dyed eggs, a rice wine herbal brew, and pickled trotters and ginger. Still a little boy, I was told pig's trotters promoted lactation and that this piquant, pickled dish was especially good for women who had just given birth.

Regardless of its tonic effects, this dish makes a delightful appetizer. Lovers of trotters will readily appreciate its virtues, and those who try it for the first time will be impressed by how such lowly ingredients become so palatable. It is the ginger that mellows the vinegar. When you buy the pig's trotters, get the more meaty hind pair. Enjoy this dish hot or at room temperature, and it may be made a day or two in advance.

METHOD

Blanch the trotters in boiling hot water for 30 minutes. Drain well.

In a medium-sized pot, combine the vinegar, ginger, and sugar. Bring the mixture to a boil and add the trotters. Turn the heat to low, cover, and gently simmer for 2 hours or until tender. Serve hot or at room temperature.

POULTRY

Qiguo Ji

YUNNAN STEAMED POT CHICKEN

**SERVES 4 TO 6 AS PART
OF A CHINESE MEAL, OR 4
AS A SINGLE DISH**

---

4 lb/ 1.8 kg chicken, cut
into pieces

---

1 tsp salt

---

6 slices of fresh ginger
root

---

2 spring onions cut into
2 in/ 5 cm pieces

---

1 ¼ pints/ 700 ml
chicken stock

---

2 tbsp rice wine

Dipping sauces

---

light soy sauce

---

chili bean sauce

---

chopped spring onions

The original version of this recipe calls for white Chinese fungus which is rarely available in the West. To make it I use a Yunnan ceramic steam pot, a squat, round, lidded vessel with an internal spout that allows steam to circulate but not to escape. Steaming in a covered heat-proof casserole for 2 hours will do almost as well. The steaming broth gently bathes the chicken pieces in a rich and flavorful atmosphere that permeates the meat. Chicken steamed this way produces a superior clear soup enriched by condensation of the natural juices of the bird. Serve the soup accompanied by a platter of chicken with dipping sauces.

METHOD

Blanch the chicken for 3 minutes in a large pot of boiling water. Remove the chicken and rinse thoroughly in cold running water. Place the chicken pieces around the Yunnan pot or on a rack set into a heat-proof casserole. Sprinkle the chicken with the salt, and scatter the ginger pieces and onions over the top. Pour in the chicken stock and rice wine or sherry. Cover and gently steam for 2 hours, replenishing the hot water from time to time if needed.

Remove the ginger and onion pieces. With a spoon, skim off all the surface fat. Ladle the soup into a tureen, and pass the chicken on a platter with the selection of dipping sauces.

Huo Zhong Dun Ji Tang

STEWED CHICKEN WITH SMOKED HAM KNUCKLE

T he nutritious, the medicinal and the flavorful are often joined in Chinese cuisine. Pig's trotters and chicken are both believed to be good for the blood and circulation. I say that the warming richness of this stew is good for whatever may ail you. It can be made ahead of time as it reheats perfectly.

METHOD

Have your butcher cut the ham knuckle in 4 pieces. Wash the pieces in cold running water until cleaned. Place them in a bowl, cover completely with cold water, and soak for 8 hours or overnight.

Place the pieces of ham knuckle in a large pot of boiling water and blanch for 5 minutes. Remove them and drain well. Discard the water and wash the pot thoroughly. Put the ham, ginger, whole onions, rice wine or sherry, salt and water in the pot and bring the mixture to a boil. Turn the heat to low, cover, and slowly cook for 1 hour.

Cut the chicken into quarters and blanch them in a large pot of boiling water for 5 minutes. Drain well and set aside.

Cut the Chinese cabbage into thick 1 × 3 in/ 25 mm × 7.5 cm strips. When the meat is tender, add the chicken and cabbage, then add the second batch of ginger, onions, rice wine or sherry, and salt. Cover and cook over low heat for another hour. Skim off all surface fat and remove the ginger and onions. Season to taste with salt and pepper. Ladle into a large bowl and serve at once.

SERVES 4 TO 6 AS PART OF A CHINESE MEAL, OR 4 AS A SINGLE DISH

1 ½ lb/ 700 g smoked ham knuckle

4 slices fresh ginger root

4 whole spring onions

2 tbsp rice wine or dry sherry

1 tsp salt

3 pints/ 1.7 litres water

3 ½–4 lb/ 1.6–1.8 kg chicken

1 lb Chinese cabbage

4 slices fresh ginger root

4 spring onions, white parts only

3 tbsp rice wine or dry sherry

1 tsp salt

salt and pepper

Mati Jiding

SPICY CHICKEN WITH FRESH WATER CHESTNUTS

8 oz/ 225 g boneless chicken breast, skinned

1 egg white

1 tsp salt

2 tsp cornflour

8 oz/ 225 g water chestnuts, fresh or canned

4 fl oz/ 125 ml peanut oil

1 tbsp finely chopped garlic

2 tsp finely chopped peeled fresh ginger root

1 tbsp chili bean sauce

2 tsp dark soy sauce

2 tsp rice wine or dry sherry

2 tsp sugar

½ tsp salt

2 tsp sesame oil

Famished one day while on a train trip from Hangzhou to Suzhou, I had to risk the dining car's offerings. To my surprise, I savored a dish of bits of chicken and water chestnuts in a spicy, very pleasing sauce. It is easy to make, as befits a dining car speciality.

METHOD

Cut the chicken into ½ in/ 12 mm dice. Combine it with the egg white, salt and cornflour in a small bowl and put the mixture into the refrigerator for about 20 minutes. If you are using fresh water chestnuts, peel them. If you are using canned water chestnuts, drain them well and rinse in cold water. Coarsely chop the water chestnuts.

Heat a wok or large frying pan until hot and add the oil. When it is moderately hot, add the diced chicken and stir well to keep it from sticking. When the chicken pieces turn white, about 2 minutes, quickly drain the chicken and all the oil into a stainless steel colander set in a bowl.

Clean the wok or pan and reheat. Return 2 tablespoons of oil to the wok, add the garlic and ginger and stir-fry for 30 seconds. Then add the water chestnuts, chili bean sauce, soy sauce, rice wine or sherry, sugar and salt and continue to stir-fry for 1 minute. Return the chicken to the wok and continue to cook for another 2 minutes. Add the sesame oil, give the mixture a final stir, and serve at once.

Hongshao Ruge

CRISPY ROAST SQUAB

J ustly famed for their skill in cooking small birds, the Cantonese overcame the problem of there being so many small bones by cutting the birds into bite-sized morsels before serving them. Diners can then easily extract the meat.

In this recipe, the squab are not really roasted. They are quickly cooked in a flavorful liquid, dried, and then, just before serving, dropped into very hot oil to finish the cooking. Their skin becomes crisp, with a lacquered look, while the meat remains tender, juicy, and flavorful. The preparation takes a little time but the first steps may be done well in advance. The result is well worth the effort and makes a terrific first course.

METHOD

Blanch the squabs in a large pot of salted boiling water for 2 minutes and remove them with a slotted spoon. Drain well.

In a medium-sized pot, combine the braising liquid ingredients and bring the mixture to a simmer. Add the squabs, cover, and simmer for 20 minutes. Remove the squabs and allow to dry thoroughly, about 1 hour. The recipe can be made to this point up to 4 hours ahead.

Just before serving, heat a wok or large frying pan until hot. Add the oil and when it is medium hot, deep-fry the squabs until they are crispy and brown. Drain them on kitchen towels, cut them into bite-sized pieces and serve at once.

SERVES 4 AS PART OF A CHINESE MEAL, OR 2 AS A SINGLE DISH

2 squabs, each about 12 oz–1 lb/ 350–450 g

Braising liquid

2 fresh ginger root slices

3 whole spring onions

3 tbsp light soy sauce

2 tbsp dark soy sauce

2 tbsp rice wine or dry sherry

2 tbsp sugar

1 tbsp honey

1 tsp salt

1 ¼ pints/ 700 ml chicken stock

16 fl oz/ 450 ml peanut oil

Donggu Shao Ji

CHICKEN AND MUSHROOM CASSEROLE

**SERVES 4 AS PART OF A
CHINESE MEAL, OR 2 AS A
SINGLE DISH**

1 lb/ 450 g boned
chicken thigh meat, skin
removed

Marinade

1 tbsp light soy sauce

2 tsp rice wine or dry
sherry

1 tsp dark soy sauce

1 tsp sesame sauce

½ tsp salt

1 tsp cornflour

1 oz/ 25 g Chinese dried
black mushrooms

2 tbsp peanut oil

6 slices fresh peeled
ginger

1 tbsp rice wine or dry
sherry

1 tbsp dark soy sauce

1 tsp light soy sauce

2 tsp sugar

8 fl oz/ 225 ml chicken
stock

There are more varieties of fresh mushrooms in the markets of Yunnan than in any other region of China. The province produces over two hundred edible varieties, many of which are similar to the French cèpe. Another kind, the oyster mushroom, is now cultivated widely outside China. But the most famous of the Yunnan mushrooms is the Jizong, or the "chicken mushroom", so called because its shape resembles a cock's comb and because its texture is like that of chicken. Not surprisingly, it is often used in chicken recipes.

In this hearty mushroom and chicken casserole, I have substituted black mushrooms, since the Yunnan variety is not often available outside of the Kunming area. The rich smoky flavor of these mushrooms is quite delicious in this dish.

METHOD

Cut the meat into thin slices about 3 in/ 7.5 cm long. In a medium-sized bowl, combine the marinade ingredients and the chicken and let them sit for 20 minutes.

Soak the mushrooms in warm water for 20 minutes or until they are soft. Rinse under running water to remove any remaining sand. With a sharp knife, remove the stems and discard. Cut the caps in half and set aside.

Heat a wok or large frying pan until hot. Add the oil and ginger slices and stir-fry for 1 minute. Then add the chicken and stir-fry for 2 minutes. Pour the contents into a clay pot or casserole, together with the mushrooms, rice wine or

sherry, soy sauces, sugar and chicken stock. Bring
the mixture to a boil, lower the heat, cover and
simmer for 15 minutes. Remove the cover and
pour in the cornflour mixture. Cook until the
sauce thickens, about 2 minutes. Remove the
ginger slices before serving.

1 tsp cornflour mixed
with 1 tsp water

Yunnan Kao Ya

YUNNAN ROAST DUCK

**SERVES 6 TO 8 AS PART
OF A CHINESE MEAL, OR 2
TO 4 AS A SINGLE DISH**

3 ½–4 lb/ 1.6–1.8 kg
whole duck, fresh or
frozen

Salt and freshly ground
black pepper

1 ½ pint/ 850 ml water

3 tbsp dark soy sauce

3 tbsp honey

2 tbsp white rice vinegar

Dipping condiments

5 tbsp hoisin sauce
mixed with 2 tbsp chili
bean sauce

2 tbsp salt mixed with
2 tsp freshly ground
black pepper

6 spring onions, cut into
2 in/ 5 cm pieces

E very region of China has its duck speciality, and Yunnan is no exception. In the Yunnan countryside, roadside restaurants display ducks, cooked and uncooked, hanging from poles outside. Brick and clay ovens are kept going day and night, cooking even more ducks. The Yunnan method of preparation follows the typical Chinese technique: the ducks are basted and hung out for hours to dry in the breeze, a necessary step before roasting to produce crispy skin and moist meat. What makes eating duck in Yunnan unique is the combination of condiments and seasonings used as dipping sauces: sweet bean sauce with chili, a salt-and-pepper mixture which uses black instead of Sichuan peppercorns, and spring onion morsels are all served. To my surprise, no flour pancakes or steamed wheat buns came with the duck. Served simply with plain rice, this dish makes an excellent centerpiece for a special dinner party.

METHOD

If the duck is frozen, thaw it thoroughly. Rinse the duck well and blot it completely dry with kitchen paper and season the cavity with salt and pepper. Then insert a meat hook near the neck.

Combine the water, soy sauce, honey and vinegar in a large pot and bring the mixture to a boil. Using a large ladle, baste the duck several times until all the skin has been completely coated with the mixture. Hang the duck in a cool, well-ventilated place to dry or, alternatively, hang it in front of a fan for about 4 to 5 hours, longer if possible. Once the duck has dried, the surface of the skin will feel like parchment.

Preheat the oven to No 9/ 475°F/ 240°C. Place the duck on a roasting rack in a roasting pan, breast side up. Pour 4 fl oz/ 125 ml water into the roasting pan. Put the duck into the oven and roast for 15 minutes, then turn down the heat to No 4/ 350°F/ 180°C and continue to roast for 50 minutes. The skin will be a deep mahogany color and very crisp when the duck is done. Meanwhile, prepare the dipping condiments.

Remove the duck from the oven and let it sit for 10 minutes, then cut it for serving. Using a cleaver or sharp knife, cut the duck into serving pieces by first dividing it into quarters, and then cutting the quarters into bite-sized pieces. Serve at once with the sauces.

Huaqi Shen Dun Ruge

SQUAB SOUP WITH GINSENG

SERVES 4 TO 6 AS PART OF A CHINESE MEAL, OR 4 AS A SINGLE DISH

2 squabs, each about 12 oz–1 lb/ 350–450 g

2 ½ pints/ 1.4 litres chicken stock

2 slices fresh ginger root

4 spring onions, white part only

1 oz/ 25 g ginseng root

2 tbsp rice wine or dry sherry

2 tsp salt

freshly ground white pepper to taste

2 tsp sesame oil

Ginseng is the most celebrated medicinal herb among Chinese everywhere. No other natural product can match its reputed healing powers. Ginseng, it is believed, imparts energy, assists the body's natural healing powers, increases one's efficiency, and tranquilizes the soul.

It's mysterious to me how the price of ginseng is determined. Some ginseng costs only a few dollars a root, while another root, looking much the same and, I am sure, exactly the same chemically, will cost thousands. Geography does play a role because ginseng from northern China commands the most money. According to legend, those at death's door who drink a brew of ginseng from the north recover immediately and live long, healthy lives.

In any case, this aromatic relative of wild sarsaparilla imparts a certain *je ne sais quoi* to any dish, especially one like this which combines some rather hearty flavors.

METHOD

Blanch the squabs in a large pot of boiling water for 3 minutes.

In a large pot, combine the chicken stock, squab, ginger and onions and bring the mixture to a boil. Turn the heat down, cover, and simmer for 2 hours. Add the ginseng and cook for 1 more hour.

Remove the ginger, onions, and skim off all surface fat. Add the rice wine or sherry, salt, pepper and sesame oil. Stir the soup and serve at once.

FISH AND SHELLFISH

Zao Liu Yu Pian

STIR-FRIED FISH FILLETS WITH CLOUD EARS AND CUCUMBERS

SERVES 4 AS PART OF A CHINESE MEAL, OR 2 AS A SINGLE DISH

1 ½ lb/ 700 g thick-cut fillets of any firm, white-fleshed fish such as cod, halibut, scrod or red snapper, or 1 ¾ lb/ 800 g fish steaks on the bone

2 tsp salt

2 tbsp light soy sauce

1 tbsp rice wine or dry sherry

2 tsp cornflour

1 oz cloud ear fungus

8 oz/ 225 g cucumber, about 1

3 tbsp peanut oil

½ tbsp finely chopped peeled garlic

1 tbsp finely chopped peeled fresh ginger root

1 ½ tbsp rice wine or dry sherry

2 tbsp light soy sauce

1 tbsp dark soy sauce

8 fl oz/ 225 ml chicken stock

S tudents of Chinese cuisine know, and countless of its recipes illustrate, that China could be called the land of mushrooms. The commercial cultivation of mushrooms began in China around the mid-seventh century AD, about one thousand years before European cultivation began in France. There are about three hundred kinds of mushrooms to be found in China; eighty-three of these varieties are known to be poisonous.

In this recipe, "cloud ears", a smaller version of the popular wood ear fungus, lend their subtle earthy flavor and distinctive texture to the dish. The crunchy cucumbers add another texture and complement the delicately flavored fillets. In China, I enjoyed this dish made with fresh carp fillets but any firm, white-fleshed fish will work as well.

METHOD

Cut the fillets into 2 in/ 5 cm long and 1 in/ 25 mm wide pieces. Put them into a bowl with the salt, soy sauce, rice wine or sherry, and cornflour and mix well. Let the fillets marinate for 1 hour.

Soak the cloud ear fungus in warm water for at least 15 minutes. Rinse them several times in cold running water to remove any sand. Drain thoroughly and set aside.

Peel the cucumber, slice it in half lengthwise and remove any seeds. Cut the halves into 2 in/ 5 cm long and 1 in/ 25 mm wide pieces.

Heat a wok or large frying pan until hot and add 2 tbsp of oil. Put in the fish pieces and fry them until they are lightly browned, about 2 minutes.

Remove them with a slotted spoon and drain thoroughly on kitchen paper.

Reheat the wok or pan and add the remaining oil. When the oil is hot, add the cloud ear fungus, cucumber, garlic, and ginger and stir-fry for 1 minute. Add the rice wine or sherry, soy sauces, and chicken stock and cook for 3 minutes. Add the cornflour mixture and stir. Return the fish pieces to the wok and cook gently until the fish is heated through. Ladle onto a platter and serve with rice.

2 tsp cornflour mixed
with 1 tbsp water

Qing Zheng Yu

STEAMED FISH SOUTHERN STYLE

SERVES 4 AS PART OF A CHINESE MEAL, OR 2 AS A SINGLE DISH

2–2 ½ lb/ 900 g–1.1 kg firm, white-fleshed fresh fish such as a small cod, halibut, haddock, scrod or red snapper, or a sole, cleaned and left whole.

1 tsp salt

3 slices of peeled fresh ginger root, cut into shreds

2 tbsp light soy sauce

4 spring onions, finely shredded

2 tbsp peanut oil

Having seen their fish swimming around in a tank or pond only minutes before they eat it, the Cantonese know how fresh it is. While few of us in the West are so lucky, we can best enjoy the flavour of fresh fish by cooking it whole. Steaming them this easy Cantonese way ensures that the delicate flesh remains moist and the result is an elegant main course.

METHOD

Make three or four shallow slashes on each side of the fish. Rub the fish on both sides with the salt and let it sit for 20 minutes. Blanch the fish in a large pot of boiling water for 2 minutes. Drain the fish well and put it on a heat-proof platter. Scatter the ginger shreds over the fish.

Set up a large Chinese steamer or put a rack into a wok, fish kettle or other deep pot. Fill it with about 2 in/ 5 cm of hot water. Bring the water simmer. Put the platter with the fish into the steamer or onto the rack. Cover the steamer tightly and gently steam over medium heat for 20 minutes.

Remove the platter with the cooked fish from the steamer and pour off all the liquid. Pour the soy sauce over the fish and scatter the onions over and around the fish. Heat the oil until it just smokes, pour this over the fish and serve at once.

Li Yu

MANDARIN FISH

SERVES 4 AS PART OF A
CHINESE MEAL, OR 2 AS A
SINGLE DISH

With all its rivers and lakes, China is blessed with a great variety of such fish as the Mandarin and the carp. I sampled this recipe at a local restaurant in Shaoxing. Steaming preserves the delicate freshwater flavors and the famous local rice wine provides the basis for the rich sauce. With the mushrooms and bamboo shoots, this dish makes a substantial and flavorful meal, a centerpiece for any family gathering. In the absence of the Mandarin this recipe works well with any firm, white fish.

1 oz/ 25 g Chinese black dried mushrooms

1-1 ½ lb/ 450-700 g firm, white-fleshed fish such as a small cod, halibut, haddock, scrod or red snapper, or sole, cleaned and left whole

1 tsp salt

3 tbsp dried rice wine or dry sherry

2 tsp light soy sauce

2 tsp sugar

METHOD

Soak the mushrooms for 20 minutes in warm water. Remove the stems and finely shred the caps.

Make three or four slashes on each side of the fish to help it cook faster and allow the flavors to permeate. Rub the fish on both sides with the salt. Set on a heatproof platter. Combine the rice wine or sherry, soy sauce, and sugar and pour over the fish. Scatter the bamboo shoots, mushrooms and ginger over and around the fish.

1 oz/ 25 g finely shredded canned bamboo shoots

3 slices of fresh ginger, shredded

1 tsp cornflour mixed with 2 tsp water

Set up a steamer or put a rack into a wok or deep pan. Fill the steamer with about 2 in/ 5 cm of hot water. Bring the water to a simmer. Put the plate with the fish into the steamer or onto the rack. Cover the steamer tightly and gently steam the fish until it is cooked. Flat fish will take about 6 minutes. Thicker fish such as sea bass will take about 15 to 18 minutes.

Remove the plate of cooked fish and pour all of the liquid into a small pan. Bring this to a simmer and add the cornflour mixture. When the sauce has thickened, pour it over the fish and serve at once.

Xi Hu Cu Yu

WEST LAKE CARP IN VINEGAR SAUCE

**SERVES 4 AS PART OF A
CHINESE MEAL, OR 2 AS A
SINGLE DISH**

2 ½–3 lb/ 1.1–1.4 kg
fresh whole carp or
catfish or 3 fresh whole
trout

2 tbsp rice wine or dry
sherry

3 tbsp light soy sauce

1 tsp of salt

2 tbsp peanut oil

2 tbsp finely chopped
peeled fresh ginger root

3 tbsp finely chopped
spring onions

3 tbsp black rice vinegar

2 tsp rice wine or dry
sherry

2 tbsp sugar

2 tbsp dark soy sauce

4 fl oz/ 125 ml chicken
stock

2 tsp cornflour mixed
with 2 tsp water

Carp have been domesticated and kept in ponds for many centuries in China. Valued for their golden scales as well as for their tasty flesh, they have a distinctive, rich, strong flavor. The Chinese use rice wine or vinegar or a combination to bring zest to the rich flesh. I enjoyed this dish in a restaurant in the city of Hangzhou, famous for its West Lake where the carp come from, and also near Shaoxing, the rice wine area.

It is no accident that this recipe calls for rice wine and rice vinegar. Zhejiang province surrounding the city is famous for both but especially for its black vinegar. The vinegar is used by itself most often as a dipping sauce for the local freshwater hairy crabs. When used with wine, as in this recipe, the result is a subtle, sweet and sour, dark, rich sauce which makes a perfect complement for the carp. If carp is unavailable, catfish or trout make acceptable substitutes.

METHOD

Have the fishmonger clean and scale the fish. Rinse the fish under cold running water and then pat it completely dry. Make four diagonal slashes across each side of the fish. In a small bowl, mix together the rice wine or sherry, soy sauce and salt, and rub evenly over both sides of the fish. Set aside for 10 minutes.

Heat a wok or large frying pan until hot, and add the oil, ginger and spring onions. Stir-fry for 30 seconds, then add the vinegar, rice wine or sherry, sugar, soy sauce and stock. Bring the mixture to a simmer and pour in the cornflour mixture.

Pour the sauce into a saucepan and keep warm.

Clean the wok or pan, fill it with water, and bring it to a simmer. Carefully lower the fish into the water and simmer for 5 minutes. Turn off the heat and let the fish steep in the hot water for 5 more minutes. If you are using trout, reduce the cooking and steeping times to 3 minutes each. Remove the fish with a slotted spoon or spatula and drain well. Place the fish on a platter, pour over the sauce and serve at once.

Hongshao Wanyu

RED-COOKED GRASS CARP WITH TANGERINE PEEL

SERVES 4 AS PART OF A CHINESE MEAL, OR 2 AS A SINGLE DISH

½ oz/ 15 g dried tangerine or citrus peel

---

2 ½–3 lb/ 1.1–1.4 kg firm, white-fleshed fish such as carp, rock fish, cod, halibut, haddock, scrod or red snapper, or sole, cleaned and left whole

---

2 tsp salt

---

4 tbsp cornflour

---

16 fl oz/ 450 ml peanut oil

---

2 tbsp finely chopped garlic

---

3 tbsp finely chopped peeled fresh ginger root

---

4 tbsp finely chopped spring onions

---

3 tbsp rice wine or dry sherry

---

1 tbsp whole bean sauce (yellow bean sauce)

---

2 tbsp dark soy sauce

---

1 tbsp sugar

---

6 tbsp chicken stock or water

'Red cooking' means braising with a strong, reddish sauce. The technique is usually applied to meat but it works well with any fresh, firm white fish.

METHOD

Soak the tangerine or citrus peel for 20 minutes in warm water or until it is soft. Rinse under running water, squeeze out any excess liquid, finely chop, and set aside.

Make three or four slashes on each side of the fish to help it cook faster and allow the flavors to penetrate. Rub the fish on both sides with the salt. Sprinkle the cornflour evenly on each side of the fish.

Heat a wok or deep frying pan until hot. Add the oil, and when it is hot, deep-fry the fish on each side for 5 to 8 minutes until it is brown and crispy. Remove the fish and drain on kitchen paper.

Pour off most of the oil, leaving 2 tablespoons, and reheat the wok or pan. Add the chopped tangerine peel, garlic, ginger and spring onions and stir-fry for 30 seconds. Put in the rest of the ingredients. Return the fish to the pan, spooning the ingredients over the top of the fish. Cover and cook over low heat for 8 minutes. When the fish is cooked, carefully remove it to a serving platter and serve at once.

You Bao Xia

OIL-EXPLODED PRAWNS

I enjoyed this austere but elegant dish at a popular Shanghai restaurant. It is usually made with unpeeled freshwater prawns that almost literally explode when they come into contact with the very hot oil in the wok. Quick cooking and light seasonings preserve and enhance the natural flavors of the prawns. When freshwater prawns are unavailable, the saltwater variety are a good substitute.

METHOD

If the prawns are unpeeled, peel them by removing their shell, legs and tail. Devein them by making a surface cut down the back of the prawns and removing the black, green or yellow matter. Rinse them well under cold running water and pat them thoroughly dry with kitchen paper. Rub the prawns evenly with salt and cornflour.

Heat a wok or large frying pan until hot and add the oil. Put in the prawns and stir-fry for 1 minute. Add the rice wine or sherry, stir, and then pour in the cornflour mixture and continue to stir-fry another 2 minutes. Serve at once.

SERVES 4 AS PART OF A CHINESE MEAL, OR 2 AS A SINGLE DISH

1 lb/ 450 g medium-sized raw prawns with shells but without heads, or 12–13 oz/ 350–375 g peeled, raw prawns

1 tsp salt

2 tsp cornflour

2 tbsp peanut oil

2 tbsp rice wine or dry sherry

1 tsp cornflour mixed with 2 tsp water

Bai Zhuo Jiwei Xia

WHITE-BLANCHED PRAWNS

SERVES 4 AS PART OF A CHINESE MEAL, OR 2 AS A SINGLE DISH

1 lb/ 450 g medium-sized fresh raw prawns, unpeeled

2 tsp salt

Dipping sauce

2 tbsp light soy sauce

1 tbsp dark soy sauce

2 spring onions, finely shredded

1 ½ tbsp peanut oil

Using the freshest possible prawns is essential for this dish. For finicky chefs in Hong Kong or Guangzhou, both close to the China Sea, this is not a problem. Another imperative is never to overcook the prawns; they must be plucked from the hot boiling water at just the right second to retain their flavor.

In Hong Kong, the prawns are served with a fresh chili dipping sauce, but I prefer this version from a Guangzhou restaurant. It's a simple mixture of soy, spring onion and hot oil, and can be served as an impressive starter.

METHOD

Rinse the prawns well under cold running water. Blot them completely dry with kitchen paper and set aside.

Mix the soy sauces and onion shreds in a small saucer. Heat the oil until it is smoking and pour this over the spring onion mixture.

Bring a large pot of water to a boil and add the salt. Add all the prawns at once and cook for 4 minutes. Remove them immediately with a slotted spoon, arrange on a platter, and serve at once with the dipping sauce.

Long Jing Chao Xia

PRAWNS IN DRAGON WELL TEA

I have heard about this dish since I was a child: freshwater prawns stir-fried and uniquely flavored by the legendary Long Jing (Dragon Well) teas of Zhejiang province. Connoisseurs of Chinese tea regard Dragon Well as the finest. The leaves of this green tea are prepared in a complex process that avoids fermentation. The best quality leaves are picked before the spring rains fall and when the young stems have but one tender sprout. These fragile sprouts are the basis for the tea's delicate and refreshing fragrance and taste. Even more common Chinese green teas will produce wonderful results.

METHOD

If the prawns are unpeeled, peel them by removing their shell, legs and tail. Devein them by making a surface cut down the back of the prawns and removing the black, green or yellow matter. Rinse them well under cold running water and pat them thoroughly dry with kitchen towels. Rub the prawns evenly with salt and set aside.

Put the tea leaves in a heat-proof measuring cup and pour in the hot water. Let the tea steep for 15 minutes.

Heat a wok or large frying pan until hot and add the oil. Then add the prawns and rice wine or sherry and stir-fry for 30 seconds. Pour in the tea and half of the leaves and cook for another minute. Remove the prawns with a slotted spoon to a serving platter and reduce any liquid in the wok by half. Pour this over the prawns and serve at once.

SERVES 4 AS PART OF A CHINESE MEAL, OR 2 AS A SINGLE DISH

1 lb/ 450 g medium-sized raw prawns, unpeeled with heads removed, or 12 to 13 ounces, peeled, raw prawns

2 tsp salt

1 tbsp Long Jing (Dragon Well) Tea or any Chinese green tea

8 fl oz/ 225 ml boiling water

1 ½ tbsp peanut oil

1 tbsp rice wine or dry sherry

Chao Manli Xiaren Mian

STIR-FRIED EELS WITH PRAWNS IN NOODLE SOUP

SERVES 4 IN CHINESE MEAL, OR 2 AS SINGLE DISH

---

8 oz/ 225 g fresh eel fillets

---

1 tsp salt

---

1 tsp sesame oil

---

1 tsp cornflour

---

8 oz/ 225 g medium-sized uncooked prawns, peeled

---

1 lb/ 450 g fresh Chinese noodles

---

1 ½ pint/ 850 g chicken stock

---

1 ½ tbsp peanut oil

---

2 tbsp finely chopped spring onions

---

1 tbsp finely chopped peeled fresh ginger root

---

2 tbsp rice wine or dry sherry

---

2 tsp light soy sauce

---

2 tsp sugar

---

1 tsp salt

---

1 tsp cornflour mixed with 2 tsp water

---

1 tbsp sesame oil

All noodle soups in China use fresh ingredients, and this desire for freshness might disturb Western sensibilities. Eels, for example, harvested from nearby rivers, are kept alive at food stalls until ready for cooking. High in protein and inexpensive, eel adds a great deal to the humble noodle soups that the Chinese so love. This is my version of a dish I had in Hangzhou. If fresh eel is not available, use any firm, white fish fillets such as cod, halibut, haddock, scrod, red snapper or sole.

METHOD

Cut the eel or fish fillets into long, thin 3 × ¼ in/ 7.5 cm × 6 mm strips. Combine the eel with the salt, sesame oil and cornflour and set aside. Blanch the prawns in a pot of salted, boiling water for 45 seconds. Drain thoroughly and set aside.

Blanch the noodles in a pot of boiling water for 2 minutes. Drain thoroughly and set aside.

In a large pot, bring the stock to a simmer.

Heat a wok or large frying pan until hot. Add the oil, onions and ginger and stir-fry for 15 seconds. Then add the fish and prawns and gently stir-fry for 2 minutes. Add the rice wine or sherry, soy sauce, sugar and salt and stir-fry another minute, making sure to combine them well. Pour in the cornflour mixture and when it has thickened, remove from the heat.

Place the noodles in a very large bowl, add the stock, then the fish and prawns mixture and drizzle over the sesame oil. Serve at once.

VEGETABLES

Jin Gu Yin Liu

STIR-FRIED BEAN SPROUTS WITH LILY BUDS

SERVES 4 AS PART OF A CHINESE MEAL, OR 2 AS A SINGLE DISH

2 oz/ 50 g dried lily bud stems

1 lb/ 450 g fresh bean sprouts

1 ½ tbsp peanut oil

½ tsp salt

Pinch of freshly ground black pepper

3 tbsp rice wine or dry sherry

1 tbsp light soy sauce

2 tsp sesame oil

Lily buds are quite edible, nutritious and inexpensive. They come dried, softening nicely when soaked and stir-fried. The bean sprouts cooked with them contribute a chewy texture which adds up to a simple but splendid dish, just like this one I enjoyed at a vegetarian restaurant in Shanghai.

METHOD

Soak the lily bud stems in warm water for 20 minutes. Drain them thoroughly and cut off the hard ends.

If you wish, snap off the ends of the bean sprouts for a more finished presentation.

Heat a wok or large frying pan until hot. Add the oil and salt, then the lily bud stems and pepper. Stir-fry for 30 seconds, add the bean sprouts, and continue to stir-fry for 1 minute. Then add the rice wine or sherry and soy sauce and continue to stir-fry for 3 minutes. Stir in the sesame oil and serve at once.

Qing Chao Bai Cai

STIR-FRIED BOK CHOY

Simple, dependable, tasty and refreshing: the Chinese attitude toward fresh seasoned vegetables, stir-fried immediately before serving. All Cantonese cooks understand that by skilfully using the minimum amount of oil in their heated woks, a few select seasonings, and a splash of water at just the right moment they can bring out the natural flavor of every vegetable. One of the best illustrations of this is fresh *bai cai* (bok choy). Found throughout China, it has a wonderful flavor reminiscent of spinach or Swiss chard.

SERVES 4 AS PART OF A CHINESE MEAL, OR 2 AS A SINGLE DISH

1 lb/ 450 g bok choy

1 tbsp peanut oil

2 garlic cloves, crushed

½ tsp salt

1 tbsp water

METHOD

Prepare the bok choy by removing the stalks with leaves from the stem. If the stalks are wide, split them in half. Cut the stalks with leaves into 3 in/ 7.5 cm pieces. Peel the stem and cut it thinly at a slight angle. Wash the bok choy in several changes of cold water. Drain and set aside.

Heat a wok or large frying pan until it is hot. Add the oil and garlic cloves and stir-fry for 30 seconds. Add the salt and bok choy and stir-fry for 1 minute over high heat. If the mixture seems dry, add 1 tablespoon of water. Continue stir-frying for 4 minutes. Turn onto a serving dish and serve at once.

Ji You Cai Xin

CABBAGE IN "CREAM" SAUCE

**SERVES 4 AS PART OF A
CHINESE MEAL, OR 2 AS A
SINGLE DISH**

1 lb/ 450 g Chinese
cabbage

1 ½ tbsp peanut oil

2 peeled garlic cloves,
crushed

12 fl oz/ 350 ml chicken
stock

½ tsp salt

½ tsp freshly ground
white pepper

1 tsp cornflour mixed
with 1 tsp water

egetarian dishes are common throughout China. Historic religious influences and rituals played a part, but the availability of so many different vegetables, especially soybeans, had a practical influence. In this traditional dish the Chinese cabbage is first stir-fried, then it is slowly braised in chicken stock. The stock would then be reduced, thickened, and finally enriched with chicken fat. I omit the chicken fat; the dish is tasty enough without it. The "cream" sauce is chicken stock thickened with a little cornflour. It's a humble dish, but one worthy of the Imperial banquet hall.

METHOD

Cut the Chinese cabbage into ¼ in/ 6 mm thick strips.

Heat a wok or large frying pan until hot. Add the oil and garlic and stir-fry for 30 seconds, then remove the garlic and discard. Put in the cabbage, stock, salt, and pepper and cook for 1 minute. Reduce the heat, cover, and cook slowly for 10 minutes or until the cabbage is tender. Remove them with a slotted spoon.

Over high heat, reduce the liquid in the wok or pan by half, add the cornflour mixture and continue to cook. Arrange the cabbage on a platter, pour over the sauce, and serve at once.

Xiami Baicai

CABBAGE WITH DRIED SHRIMP

othing evokes memories as sharply and as immediately as odors and tastes. The fragrance and taste of this spicy dish is very much like a comforting meal my mother used to make for me. She stir-fried common Chinese cabbage, the most common and cheapest Chinese vegetable, and enlivened the taste with dried shrimp. Like many peasant dishes, it is both nutritious and sustaining.

SERVES 4 AS PART OF A CHINESE MEAL, OR 2 AS A SINGLE DISH

1 oz/ 25 g dried shrimp

1 lb Chinese cabbage

2 tbsp peanut oil

2 tbsp finely chopped garlic

1 tbsp finely chopped peeled fresh ginger root

1 tbsp chili bean sauce

1 tbsp dark soy sauce

2 tsp sugar

4 fl oz/ 125 ml chicken stock

METHOD

Soak the dried shrimp in a large bowl of warm for 20 minutes, drain them thoroughly and coarsely chop them.

Cut the cabbage into long strips.

Heat a wok or large frying pan until hot and add the oil, garlic and ginger and stir-fry for 30 seconds. Then add the soaked shrimp, the cabbage, chili bean sauce, soy sauce, sugar and chicken stock. Cook over high heat for 5 minutes, stirring constantly. Turn onto a platter and serve.

Donggu Chao Cai

STIR-FRIED CABBAGE WITH MUSHROOMS

SERVES 4 AS PART OF A CHINESE MEAL, OR 2 AS A SINGLE DISH

---

1 oz/ 25 g Chinese dried black mushrooms

---

1 lb/ 450 g Chinese cabbage

---

4 oz/ 125 g bamboo shoots

---

1 ½ tbsp peanut oil

---

1 tbsp finely chopped peeled fresh ginger root

---

2 tsp rice wine or dry sherry

---

2 tsp light soy sauce

---

1 tsp dark soy sauce

½ tsp salt

---

water

---

2 tsp sesame oil

Buddhism greatly assisted in promoting vegetarianism among the Chinese. However, the religious element alone counted for little among them because the Chinese are almost without taboos when it comes to food. Rather, the Buddhist influence spread because China's chefs concocted imaginative vegetarian menus. Temple restaurants developed a large clientele, and their successes and dishes were quickly emulated by non-Buddhist restaurants. Thus was created the venerable tradition of vegetarian dishes in China, holding their own with meat and seafood dishes.

METHOD

Soak the mushrooms in warm water for 20 minutes or until they are soft. Rinse under running water to remove any remaining sand. With a sharp knife, remove the stems and discard. Finely shred the caps and set aside.

Chop the cabbage into long shreds about ¼ in/ 6 mm wide. Rinse the bamboo shoots under cold running water and finely shred them.

Heat a wok or large frying pan until hot. Add the oil and ginger and stir-fry for 20 seconds. Then add the mushrooms and bamboo shoots and continue to stir-fry for 1 minute. Add the rice wine or sherry, soy sauces and salt and continue to stir-fry for another 3 minutes or until the cabbage is cooked. Add about a tablespoon of water if necessary to keep the mixture moist. Spoon onto a platter, garnish with the sesame oil, and serve at once.

Chao Qincai

STIR-FRIED CELERY

his family dish from Sichuan is also a good one to serve guests. You can use European celery or the Chinese variety, which is smaller, slightly tougher, and with a looser stalk than the European version. It is of the same species but the product of fifteen hundred years of Oriental cultivation. In Chinese, European celery is inscrutably called "Western parsley". Certain traditionalists maintain that the European version is inadequate in Chinese recipes, but I cannot agree. Just use the freshest celery you can find of whatever provenance.

SERVES 4 AS PART OF A CHINESE MEAL, OR 2 AS A SINGLE DISH

1 ½ lb/ 700 g Chinese celery or European celery

2 tbsp peanut oil

1 tsp salt

3 tbsp finely chopped garlic

4 fl oz/ 125 ml chicken stock

METHOD

Separate the stalks of the celery from the center and with a sharp knife, remove the strings from the tougher outside stalks. Then cut the celery into 1 in/ 25 mm lengths.

Heat a wok or large frying pan until hot. Add the oil, salt and garlic and stir fry for 20 seconds. Put in the celery and continue to stir-fry for 2 minutes. Finally, pour in the chicken stock and continue to cook until most of the liquid has evaporated. Serve at once.

Ganbian Kugua

STIR-FRIED BITTER MELON WITH FRESH MILD CHILIES

SERVES 4 AS PART OF A CHINESE MEAL, OR 2 AS A SINGLE DISH

1 ½ lb/ 700 g bitter lemon

8 oz/ 225 g fresh mild chilies

1 ½ tbsp peanut oil

Pinch of salt

1 ½ tbsp chopped garlic

8 fl oz/ 225 ml chicken stock

2 tbsp light soy sauce

2 tsp sugar

Sichuan cuisine is noted for many sterling attributes, the most famous perhaps being its imaginative use of sharp, spicy flavors. An example of this is a bitter melon dish from Chengdu, Sichuan. It offers a delicious and bracing contrast of fresh whole chilies and the refreshing, cooling taste of the melon.

Most often used in soups and stir-fried dishes, bitter melon was originally deemed a medicine and was supposed to clear the blood. (Eaten without blanching to reduce its bitterness one can well understand its reputation.) Like other edible medicines, it worked its way into the culinary repertory and is now a popular food item. The ones I sampled had just been harvested, fully grown but quite green. Even with blanching, the flesh retains its firm texture. Riper melons are somewhat less bitter and softer in texture.

METHOD

Wash, then cut the bitter melon in half lengthwise and remove the seeds. Cut the melon into fine slices and blanch them in a pot of boiling water for 2 minutes. Remove with a slotted spoon and drain well on kitchen paper.

Cut the fresh chilies in half and remove the seeds. Finely slice the chilies.

Heat a wok or large frying pan over high heat and add the oil. When hot, add the salt and the chilies and stir-fry for 10 seconds. Put in the bitter melon, garlic, chicken stock, soy sauce and sugar. Turn down the heat and simmer the mixture for 3 minutes. Serve at once.

Yuxiang Qiezi

FISH-FLAVORED AUBERGINES WITH PORK

T his dish does not taste "fishy", but it does use the spices and seasonings usually employed when preparing fish: hot, sour, salty and sweet at the same time. It sounds (and tastes) very Sichuan and indeed it is. This delightful version from Sichuan uses whole aubergines. The smaller variously colored varieties used in China are generally the tastiest.

METHOD

If using ordinary aubergines, cut into quarters lengthwise. Heat a wok or large frying pan until hot. Add the oil, and when it is hot, deep-fry the aubergines whole. Remove them with a slotted spoon and drain them on kitchen paper. Arrange them on a serving platter.

Pour off most of the oil, leaving 3 tablespoons, and reheat the wok. Add the pork, garlic, ginger and spring onions and stir-fry for 30 seconds. Put in the rest of the ingredients, except the stock. Continue to cook for 2 minutes over high heat, then add the stock and simmer for another 3 minutes.

Add the aubergines and simmer in the sauce for 3 minutes and serve at once.

SERVES 4 AS PART OF A CHINESE MEAL, OR 2 AS A SINGLE DISH

1 ½ lb/ 700 g Chinese or regular aubergines

16 fl oz/ 450 ml peanut oil

1 lb/ 450 g minced pork

2 tbsp finely chopped garlic

2 tbsp finely chopped ginger root

3 tbsp finely chopped spring onions

2 tbsp dark soy sauce

3 tbsp rice wine or dry sherry

3 tbsp Chinese black rice vinegar

2 tbsp sugar

1 tbsp Sichuan peppercorns, roasted and crushed

2 tsp ground red chili

4 fl oz/ 125 ml chicken stock

Yang Qiezi

STUFFED AUBERGINE

**SERVE 4 AS PART OF A
CHINESE MEAL, OR 2 AS A
SINGLE DISH**

Batter

4 tbsp cornflour

2 tbsp unbleached white
all-purpose flour

1 tsp baking powder

2 eggs, beaten

2 tbsp beer or water

A ubergine, of which there are many varieties, was introduced many centuries ago, probably from India. They are best eaten immediately after being picked as they can quickly become quite bitter. Stuffing adds substance to the subtle aubergine taste and frying gives them a crusty exterior. Enjoy them straight from the wok, for they tend to soften up if they sit too long, though they remain delicious. The stuffing can be made well ahead of time, but dip the vegetables in the batter only when you are about to fry them.

METHOD

In a medium-sized bowl, mix the batter ingredients until smooth and set aside to rest for 5 minutes.

In a medium-sized bowl, combine the pork, prawns, onions, soy sauce, rice wine or sherry, sesame oil, salt and pepper and mix ingredients together thoroughly.

Slice the aubergines into ¼ in/ 6 mm rounds. (If you are using the larger variety, cut them into rounds, and then quarter them.) With a knife, spread a thin layer of the meat filling on one side of an aubergine slice and place another one on top and press together like a small sandwich. Continue this procedure until you have used all the aubergine rounds.

Heat a wok or large frying pan with the oil. Using cooking tongs and chopsticks, dip the stuffed rounds into the batter and then drop each gently into the hot oil. Be careful of splatters. Place as many rounds into the wok as will fit easily on one layer. Turn them gently and fry them until they are golden brown on both sides and cooked inside, about 4 minutes. Adjust your heat to keep the oil very hot but not enough to burn the rounds. Remove the rounds with a slotted spoon and drain on kitchen paper. Cook and serve the aubergine rounds in several batches so they are always hot and crispy.

Filling

4 oz/ 125 g minced pork

4 oz/ 125 g medium-sized uncooked prawns, peeled and finely chopped

3 tbsp finely chopped spring onions

2 tbsp dark soy sauce

1 tbsp rice wine or dry sherry

1 tbsp sesame oil

1 tsp salt

1 tsp freshly ground black pepper

1 lb/ 450 g Chinese aubergines (about 4 medium-sized)

1 ½ pint/ 850 ml peanut oil

Haoyou Sigua

SILK SQUASH WITH OYSTER SAUCE

**SERVES 4 AS PART OF A
CHINESE MEAL, OR 2 AS A
SINGLE DISH**

---

1 ½ lb/ 700 g silk squash
or courgettes

---

2 tbsp peanut oil

---

2 tbsp finely chopped
shallots

---

2 garlic cloves, sliced

---

3 tbsp oyster sauce

---

4 fl oz/ 125 ml chicken
stock

Subtle flavors, delicate textures, the freshest ingredients, and just the right amount of the most appropriate seasonings – these are the virtues of classic southern Chinese cooking. Silk Squash with Oyster Sauce manifests these virtues. The squash is so named because of its soft, spongy flesh which is markedly sweeter the younger the squash. It tastes like a cross between an aubergine and a cucumber. Aubergine can be used if you are unable to find silk squash.

This recipe comes from the Qing Hui Yuan restaurant in Shunde, Canton, where silk squash is cut into larger pieces than I've seen in the same dish elsewhere.

METHOD

Peel away the tough outer skin of the silk squash and cut the flesh in half lengthwise, then into 2 in/ 5 cm pieces.

Heat a wok or large frying pan until hot and add the oil. Put in the shallots, garlic, and silk squash and stir-fry for 2 minutes. Add the oyster sauce and chicken stock and simmer uncovered until tender, about 5 minutes. Serve at once.

Lajiao Shao Sijidou

GREEN BEANS STIR-FRIED WITH CHILLI

hinese who live in the countryside understandably enjoy a greater variety of fresh produce than those living in the city, with food literally from their back yards or a few yards away in nearby fields. With little or no refrigeration, produce is eaten in season, the surplus being either dried or pickled or salted. These preserving techniques have been perfected over the course of thousands of years, retaining the nutritional qualities of foods and enhancing their flavors.

At one delightful feast in Sichuan, my hostess retrieved from the ground an earthen jar she had filled with chilies to pickle. She pounded the chilies into a paste, adding that to chopped garlic and then to stir-fried fresh seasonal vegetables, in this case, green beans. I successfully repeated the recipe, using fresh mild red chilies and adding a touch of vinegar. This is an appetizing way to enjoy green beans when they are in season. They make a lovely side dish, authentically Sichuan.

SERVES 4 AS PART OF A CHINESE MEAL, OR 2 AS A SINGLE DISH

1 lb/ 450 g green beans

4 oz/ 125 g mild red or green chilies

1 ½ tbsp peanut oil

1 ½ tbsp finely chopped garlic

1 tsp salt

2 tbsp rice wine or dry sherry

2 tsp white rice vinegar

2 tsp sugar

2 tbsp water

1 tsp ground roasted Sichuan peppercorns

METHOD

String the green beans and snap them in half. Split open the red chilies and chop them coarsely.

Heat a wok or large frying pan until hot. Add the oil, garlic and salt and stir-fry for 10 seconds. Put in the chilies and stir-fry another 30 seconds. Then add the green beans, rice wine or sherry, vinegar, sugar, and water and continue to stir-fry until tender, about 5 minutes, adding more water if necessary. When the green beans are cooked, add the peppercorns, mix well and serve at once.

Chao Doujiao

Stir-Fried Green Beans with Garlic

Serves 4 as part of a Chinese meal, or 2 as a single dish

1 lb/ 450 g Chinese long beans or any fresh green beans

1 ½ tbsp peanut oil

½ tsp salt

2 tbsp coarsely chopped garlic

1 tsp finely chopped ginger

½ cup chicken stock

C runchy, sweet green beans, stir-fried with gently pungent garlic, is another speedy dish enjoyed throughout China. It exemplifies the Chinese ideal of simple but healthy, delicious food. Several varieties of fresh green beans can be used, the most dramatic being the famous Chinese yard-long beans. Some do actually attain such a length, but are of course cut into stir-fry-size pieces.

Method

Trim the ends of the beans. If you are using Chinese long beans, cut them into 3 in lengths.

Heat a wok or large frying pan until hot, add the oil and salt, and the garlic and fresh ginger and stir-fry for 30 seconds. Add the green beans and chicken stock and continue to cook for 4 minutes or until the beans are just tender and most of the liquid has evaporated. Serve at once.

Doujiao Zai Chao Sigua Yuner

LONG BEANS STIR-FRIED WITH SILK SQUASH AND CLOUD EARS

O ne of the best vegetarian dishes I have eaten anywhere was prepared in the kitchen of my own family in Kaiping (Hoiping). It's a brilliant combination of authentically Cantonese tastes and textures. The long beans were fresh from the fields, crisp and extremely sweet, the silk squash had a soft, spongy texture and earthy flavor which was a nice contrast to its coarse skin. The cloud ears had a soft but elastic texture and subtle flavor. Quickly stir-fried with the other ingredients they made this a unique dish, good as a vegetarian main course or in combination with a meat dish.

METHOD

Soak the cloud ear fungus in warm water for at least 15 minutes. Rinse them several times in cold running water to remove any sand. Drain thoroughly and set aside.

If you are using the Chinese long beans, trim the ends and cut them into 3 in/ 7.5 cm segments. If you are using green beans, trim the ends and cut them in half.

Peel off the tough outer skin of the silk squash, or top and tail the courgettes. Cut the vegetable at a slight diagonal into 2 in/ 5 cm pieces.

Heat a wok or large frying pan until hot and add the oil. Put in the shallots, garlic, ginger, cloud ears, and long beans. Stir-fry for 1 minute, then add the silk squash or courgettes, oyster sauce, rice wine or sherry, soy sauce, salt, sugar and chicken stock. Cook over high heat, uncovered, until the vegetables are tender, about 5 minutes. Serve at once.

SERVES 4 AS PART OF A CHINESE MEAL, OR 2 AS A SINGLE DISH

1 oz/ 25 g cloud ear fungus

8 oz/ 225 g Chinese long beans or green beans

1 lb silk squash or courgettes

2 tbsp peanut oil

2 tbsp finely chopped shallots

2 tbsp coarsely chopped garlic

2 tsp finely chopped peeled fresh ginger root

2 tbsp oyster sauce

2 tbsp rice wine or dry sherry

2 tbsp light soy sauce

2 tsp salt

1 tsp sugar

4 fl oz/ 125 ml chicken stock

Chao Lajiao

STIR-FRIED WHOLE MILD CHILIES

**SERVES 4 AS PART OF A
CHINESE MEAL, OR 2 AS A
SINGLE DISH**

12 oz/ 350 g fresh whole
mild chilies, preferably
of different colors

2 tbsp peanut oil

1 tsp salt

2 tbsp chopped garlic

1 tbsp light soy sauce

2 tsp sugar

4 fl oz/ 125 ml chicken
stock

I enjoyed this wonderful dish on a train trip from Hangzhou to Suzhou, known as the Venice of China because of its canals. It was the first and only time I have ever eaten a dish composed entirely of whole cooked chilies. It worked well because the chilies were mild, fresh and in season, therefore cheap and delicious. Variously colored, the chilies – from green to yellow, orange, and bright red – were a delight to the eye.

It is interesting to note that there are over two hundred varieties of chilies, ranging in taste from mild to devilishly hot. Chilies are more than spicy; they are quite nutritious as well, being rich in vitamins A and C and in iron, calcium, and traces of other minerals. They were introduced into Asia from the New World almost five hundred years ago and were immediately assimilated into Asian cuisines. In high mountain areas of the Sichuan region where cabbages and sweet potatoes do not thrive, the chilies supply much-needed vitamins. This can be served simply with rice.

METHOD

Wash the chilies and pat them dry. Leave them whole.

Heat a wok or large frying pan over high heat. When hot, add the oil, salt and garlic. Put in the chilies and stir-fry for 1 minute. Then add the soy sauce and sugar, and pour in the chicken stock and continue to stir-fry until most of the liquid has evaporated. Pour the mixture onto a platter and serve at once.

Feicui Ji Pian

EMERALD CHICKEN "MEAT"

**SERVES 6 AS PART OF A
CHINESE MEAL, OR 3 TO 4
AS A SINGLE DISH**

8 oz/ 225 g fresh or
canned wheat gluten
(p. 145)

8 oz/ 225 g mild chilies
or green peppers

1 ½ tbsp peanut oil

1 ½ tbsp finely chopped
garlic

½ tsp salt

¼ tsp freshly ground
white pepper

4 fl oz/ 125 ml chicken
stock or water

1 ½ tbsp rice wine or dry
sherry

2 tbsp light soy sauce

½ tsp cornflour mixed
with 1 tsp water

1 tbsp sesame oil

F or many centuries in China, wheat gluten has been made into imitation meats for vegetarian styles of cooking. The Buddhist influence here is unmistakable. Wheat gluten is a nutritious, high-protein food with a texture that lends itself to imaginative uses. It has a delicate flavor of its own but readily absorbs sauces and condiments. The mild green chilies impart the "emerald" touch in this recipe from Shanghai.

One can make wheat gluten at home, but it is time-consuming. In labor-intensive China, fresh gluten is always available but the prepared variety is an acceptable substitute.

METHOD

Rinse the wheat gluten in several changes of cold water. Cut the wheat gluten in round slices and set aside.

Clean and seed the chilies or peppers and cut into similar sizes.

Heat a wok or large frying pan until hot. Add the oil, garlic, salt and white pepper. Put in the chilies or peppers and stir-fry for 30 seconds. Add the wheat gluten slices and continue to stir-fry for another minute. Pour in the chicken stock or water, rice wine or sherry and soy sauce and simmer for 3 minutes. Add the cornflour mixture and mix well. Lastly add the sesame oil and give the mixture several good stirs. Serve at once.

Yuxiang Gesong

MINCED CHILI "FISH"

**SERVES 4 AS PART OF A
CHINESE MEAL, OR 2 AS A
SINGLE DISH**

8 oz/ 225 g fresh or
canned wheat gluten

1 oz/ 25 g Chinese dried
black mushrooms,
soaked, stems removed

1 ½ tbsp peanut oil

2 tbsp finely chopped
garlic

3 tbsp finely chopped
spring onions

1 tbsp finely chopped
fresh ginger root

3 tbsp pine nuts

2 tbsp light soy sauce

2 tsp Chinese white rice
vinegar

2 tsp sugar

2 tsp chili bean sauce

½ tsp salt

½ tsp freshly ground
black pepper

6 tbsp water

½ tsp cornflour mixed
with 1 tsp water

T his recipe mimics a well-known fish dish, and it certainly fooled me. The gluten (p. 145) is cut up as if it were fish; and with the Chinese dried black mushrooms, pine nuts, and the traditional chili sauce, it resembles and tastes very much like a real fish dish.

METHOD

Rinse the wheat gluten in several changes of cold water, drain, and cut into small dice. Do the same with the mushrooms and set aside.

Heat a wok or large frying pan until hot. Add the oil, garlic, onions and ginger and stir-fry for 30 seconds. Put in the wheat gluten, mushrooms, and pine nuts. Continue to stir-fry for 1 minute, then add the rest of the ingredients except the cornflour mixture and cook for another minute. Pour in the cornflour mixture and cook until the sauce thickens. Turn the dish onto a platter and serve at once.

Qing Sun Shao Rou

STEM LETTUCE WITH CLOUD EARS

Stem lettuce is a Chinese original, found most often in the north and west. It has a quite unusual if not bizarre form, which is why it is also called "celtuce" or "asparagus lettuce". The top is in the shape of a thin oval, with wilted-looking lettuce-like leaves, while the stem is thick and crunchy, like asparagus or celery. The leaves are generally eaten in soup; the stem is often pickled. Stem lettuce can be found seasonally in Chinese food markets, though fresh broccoli stems are an acceptable substitute.

The flavors of this dish are enhanced by the touch of roasted ground Sichuan peppercorns tossed in during the last moment of cooking.

METHOD

Peel the stem lettuce or broccoli stems and cut the stems into thin slices diagonally.

Soak the cloud ear fungi in warm water for at least 15 minutes. Rinse them several times in cold running water to remove any sand. Drain thoroughly and set aside.

Heat a wok or large frying pan until hot and add the oil. Add the ginger, garlic and onions and stir-fry for 30 seconds. Put in the cloud ears and stem lettuce and stir-fry for 1 minute. Now add the chili bean sauce, rice wine or sherry, soy sauces, sugar and salt. Stir-fry for 1 minute, and then pour in the water. Continue to cook over high heat, uncovered, until the vegetables are tender, about 3 minutes. Add the peppercorns, mix well, and serve at once.

SERVES 4 AS PART OF A CHINESE MEAL, OR 2 AS A SINGLE DISH

1 lb/ 450 g stem lettuce or broccoli stems

½ oz/ 12 g cloud ear fungi

1 ½ tbsp peanut oil

1 tbsp finely chopped peeled fresh ginger root

1 tbsp finely chopped garlic

2 tbsp finely chopped green onions

2 tsp chili bean sauce

1 tbsp rice wine or dry sherry

1 tbsp light soy sauce

2 tsp dark soy sauce

1 tsp sugar

½ tsp salt

3 tbsp water

1 tsp ground roasted Sichuan peppercorns

Huangyou Xie Fen

MOCK CRAB

**SERVES 4 AS PART OF A
CHINESE MEAL, OR 2 AS A
SINGLE DISH**

8 oz/ 225 g potatoes,
peeled and cut into
small dice

8 oz/ 225 g carrots,
peeled and cut into
small dice

2 tbsp peanut oil

2 tbsp finely chopped
garlic

1 tbsp finely chopped
peeled fresh ginger root

1 tsp salt

½ tsp freshly ground
white pepper

6 eggs, beaten

1 tbsp sesame oil

A nother vegetarian dish masquerading as animal protein, this time including diced potatoes and carrots. The egg whites and shreds of yellow yolks simulate the colors of crab meat, hence the name of the dish. This is a quite flavorful simple-to-make vegetarian dish.

METHOD

Blanch the potatoes and carrots in a large pot of boiling salted water for 2 minutes and drain thoroughly.

Heat a wok or large frying pan until hot. Add the oil, garlic, ginger, salt and pepper and stir-fry for 30 seconds. Put in the carrots and potatoes, and continue to stir-fry for 1 minute.

Combine the eggs with sesame oil and pour this over the vegetables and stir. Let the mixture cook much like an omelet. When the bottom has turned to a golden brown, turn over and allow the top to brown. Slide the mock crab onto a platter and serve at once.

RICE AND NOODLES

Hua Ji Fan

CHICKEN COOKED WITH RICE

SERVES 4 AS PART OF A CHINESE MEAL, OR 2 AS A SINGLE DISH

8 oz/ 225 g long-grain white rice

8 oz/ 225 g boneless chicken thighs with skin removed

1 tbsp light soy sauce

2 tsp dark soy sauce

2 tsp rice wine or dry sherry

1 tsp salt

2 tsp sesame oil

1 tsp cornflour

1 ½ tbsp peanut oil

2 tsp finely chopped peeled fresh ginger root

Garnish

1 tbsp dark soy sauce

2 tbsp finely chopped spring onions

When my mother and I returned to our ancestral village of Kaiping (Hoiping), we were impressed to hear that my cousin's son, Tan Song-fa, was operating a successful food stall in town. It is a modest shop, with a few chairs and tables set up. It has a pleasant river view, and the air is cool, and above all, the food is cheap, simple, and deliciously satisfying.

The limited menu included spareribs with rice and yellow eel with rice, both cooked in clay pots over charcoal. The young chefs also offered quail soup, chicken soup, stir-fried preserved vegetables, and braised pig tail, all cooked on a wok heated by propane gas. It was simple fare at its best. I was especially impressed by this chicken rice dish.

METHOD

Put the rice in a clay pot or medium-sized pot. Pour in enough water to cover the rice about 1 in/ 25 mm. Bring the rice to a boil and continue to cook until most of the water has evaporated. Reduce the heat to the lowest point possible and cover tightly.

Coarsely chop the chicken and combine it with the soy sauces, rice wine or sherry, salt, sesame oil and cornflour.

Heat a wok or large frying pan until hot. Add the oil and ginger and stir-fry for 10 seconds. Then add the chicken and stir-fry for 2 minutes. Then pour the mixture on top of the rice, cover, and continue to cook for 10 minutes.

Just before serving, drizzle the soy sauce on top of the chicken and rice and garnish with the spring onions.

Yumi Zhou

RICE PORRIDGE WITH SWEETCORN

R ice since ancient times has been China's nutritious, congenially bland staple food. Sweetcorn, introduced in the early sixteenth century by Portuguese and Spanish explorers, is a relative newcomer to Chinese cuisine. Enthusiastically adopted by the people, it has become the third most important grain in the country after rice and wheat. Sweetcorn and rice cooked together make a nutritious and satisfying family-style dish. A versatile mixture, it provides a nourishing snack anytime and can also be used as a starter or main course. I sampled this version in Chengdu, Sichuan.

METHOD

Bring the water to a boil in a large pot, add the salt and then the rice. Bring back to a boil, stir several times, cover loosely, and let the rice simmer for 40 minutes at the lowest possible heat.

Add the corn and simmer for 20 more minutes. Stir in the spring onions and chili bean sauce. Before serving, sprinkle on the peppercorns.

SERVES 4 AS PART OF A CHINESE MEAL, OR 2 AS A SINGLE DISH

2 ½ pint/ 1.4 litre water

2 tsp salt

6 oz/ 175 g short-grain rice

10 oz/ 275 g fresh corn kernels (about 2 ears), or frozen corn niblets

3 tbsp finely chopped spring onions

1 tbsp chili bean sauce

Garnish

2 tsp Sichuan peppercorns, roasted and crushed

Guo Ba

SIZZLING RICE

2 oz/ 50 g Chinese dried
black mushrooms

8 oz/ 225 g lean pork

1 tbsp light soy sauce

2 tsp dark soy sauce

1 tbsp rice wine or dry
sherry

2 tsp cornflour

8 oz/ 225 g boneless
chicken breast

1 egg white

½ tsp salt

2 tsp cornflour

½ lb Chinese cabbage

1 ½ pints/ 850 ml
chicken stock

1 tsp salt

2 tbsp rice wine or dry
sherry

2 tbsp light soy sauce

1 ½ tbsp cornflour
dissolved in 2 tbsp
water

'Sizzling rice' is the term describing the minia-ture explosion that occurs when crisp hot rice collides with thick soup. The magic of having the rice sizzle as one pours the hot soup over it always delights diners. Although this popular ver-sion of the well-known rice dish is from Sichuan, it is not typically spicy. It is, however, so thick and satisfying, it may well become a meal in itself. You may make your own crisp rice at home or buy the dried rice at a Chinese grocery.

METHOD

Soak the mushrooms in warm water for 20 min-utes, squeeze out the excess liquid, cut off the stems, and quarter the caps.

Cut the pork into thin slices about ¼ in/ 6 mm thick by 2 in/ 5 cm long. Combine the pork with the soy sauces, rice wine or sherry and cornflour.

Cut the chicken into slices about ¼ in/ 6 mm thick by 2 in/ 5 cm long. Combine the chicken with the egg white, salt and cornflour and set in the refrigerator for 20 minutes.

Wash and shred the Chinese cabbage.

Bring the stock to a simmer, add the mush-rooms, cabbage, salt, rice wine or sherry, soy sauce and cornflour mixture. Simmer for 5 minutes and add the onions and sesame oil. Meanwhile, bring another pot of water to a simmer, and add the pork and chicken. Cook for 30 seconds, turn off the heat, and let the meat sit for 2 minutes. Remove the meat with a slotted spoon and add to the soup mixture.

Heat a wok or large frying pan until hot and add

the oil. When the oil is very hot, deep-fry the rice cake or crusts and drain on kitchen paper. Quickly place it or the crusts in a soup tureen or deep bowl, and pour in the soup. Serve at once.

3 tbsp finely chopped spring onions

1 tbsp sesame oil

16 fl oz/ 450 ml peanut oil

1 rice cake (p. 90) or 10 crusts of dried rice cakes

Zong Bao

DEEP-FRIED GLUTINOUS RICE CAKES

**SERVES 6 TO 8 AS
SNACKS OR AS DESSERT**
—

1 lb/ 450 g glutinous or
sweet rice
—

16 fl oz/ 450 ml water
—

1 tbsp peanut oil
—

16 fl oz/ 450 ml peanut
oil
—

sugar for dipping
—

W hile exploring the fascinating markets of the remote village of Yi Liang Gou Jie, I saw an elderly woman selling these glutinous rice cakes. She wrapped the cakes in bamboo leaves and boiled them. When a customer ordered one, she unwrapped the cake and dropped it into hot oil. It quickly puffed up and turned golden brown and crispy. She then scooped it out, drained it, and sprinkled it with sugar.

In this recipe, I cook the rice in a pot and then press it into a cake pan, bamboo leaves not always being available.

METHOD

In a large bowl, combine the rice with enough cold water to cover it at least by 2 in/ 5 cm. Soak for 8 hours or overnight. Drain well.

In a medium-sized pot, combine the rice and water. Bring the mixture to a boil, reduce the heat, cover, and cook for 40 minutes.

Using kitchen paper, rub 1 tablespoon of oil on all sides of a 8 in/ 20 cm square cake tin. Press the rice into the tin, cover it with aluminium foil, and press down on all sides until the rice is compressed as much as possible. Allow the rice to cool.

Turn the rice out onto a cutting board. It should fall out in one piece. Cut the rice into 3 × 1 ½ in/ 7.5 × 4 cm pieces.

Heat a wok or large frying pan until hot. Add the oil, and when it is hot, drop in the rice squares, a few at a time, and deep-fry until they are golden and crispy. Drain the squares thoroughly on kitchen paper. Serve warm with a dish of sugar for dipping.

Dan Dan Mian

SPICY SICHUAN NOODLES

N oodles dishes, *xiao chi*, or "small eats" are found everywhere, in hole-in-the-wall restaurants, food stalls and places selling snacks. This is a typical Sichuan dish that is now popular throughout China, especially in the north. There are many versions of it and they are all easy to make, tasty, and quite filling, but this is an exceptionally delicious one I sampled at a tiny street restaurant in Chengdu, Sichuan.

SERVES 4 TO 6 AS PART OF A CHINESE MEAL, OR 2 TO 4 AS A SINGLE DISH

8 oz/ 225 g minced pork

1 tbsp dark soy sauce

1 tsp salt

8 fl oz/ 225 ml peanut oil

3 tbsp finely chopped garlic

2 tbsp finely chopped peeled fresh ginger root

5 tbsp finely chopped spring onions

2 tbsp sesame paste or peanut butter

2 tbsp dark soy sauce

2 tbsp chili oil

2 tsp salt

8 fl oz/ 225 ml chicken stock

12 oz/ 350 g fresh Chinese thin egg noodles or dry Chinese thin egg noodles

1 tbsp Sichuan peppercorns, roasted and ground

METHOD

Combine the pork, soy sauce and salt in a small bowl and mix well. Heat a wok or frying pan until hot. Add the oil and deep-fry the pork, stirring with a spatula to break it into small pieces. When the pork is crispy and dry, about 4 minutes, remove it with a slotted spoon and drain on kitchen paper.

Pour off the oil, leaving 2 tbsp in the wok. Reheat the wok or pan and add the garlic, ginger, and onions and stir-fry for 30 seconds. Then add the sesame paste or peanut butter, soy sauce, chili oil, salt and chicken stock and simmer for 4 minutes.

Cook the noodles in a large pot of boiling water for 2 minutes if they are fresh or 5 minutes if they are dried. Drain the noodles well in a colander. Divide the noodles into individual bowls or put them in a large soup tureen. Ladle on the sauce, garnish with the fried pork and Sichuan peppercorns and serve at once.

Mayi Shang Shu

BEAN THREAD NOODLES WITH PORK

**SERVES 4 AS PART OF A
CHINESE MEAL, OR 2 AS A
SINGLE DISH**

4 oz/ 125 g dried bean
thread noodles

8 oz/ 225 g minced pork

1 tbsp dark soy sauce

2 tsp rice wine or dry
sherry

2 tsp sesame oil

1 tbsp peanut oil

1 tbsp fresh ginger root

2 tbsp garlic

4 tbsp spring onions

2 tbsp dark soy sauce

1 tbsp chili bean sauce

½ tsp salt

2 tsp sugar

2 tsp sesame oil

16 fl oz/ 450 ml chicken
stock

Garnish

3 tbsp spring onions

This classic Sichuan family dish has the rather fanciful name of Ants Climbing a Tree. When mixed with bean thread noodles, the ground pork is said to look like ants climbing a tree. It is excellent, easy, and made in a matter of minutes.

METHOD

Soak the noodles in a large bowl of warm water for 15 minutes. When they are soft, drain them and discard the water. Combine the meat with the soy sauce, rice wine or sherry, and sesame oil.

Heat a wok or large frying pan until hot. Add the peanut oil and meat mixture. Stir-fry the mixture for 2 minutes. Then add the finely chopped ginger, garlic and onions and continue to stir-fry for 2 minutes. Add the rest of the ingredients and the noodles. Bring the mixture to a simmer, mix well and cook until most of the liquid has evaporated. Ladle into a large serving bowl, garnish with finely chopped spring onions and serve.

Lianggua Rouru He

MINCED BITTER MELON WITH RICE NOODLES

T he famous Sha He restaurant attracts visitors from all over China to taste what is reputed to be the ultimate rice noodles. Located just outside the port of Guangzhou in an area renown for the quality of its rice and its water, the Sha He makes over one thousand pounds of rice noodles every day, serving them in forty different dishes. One recipe I tried marries the cool, tangy flavor of bitter melon with pork and the airy lightness of their delicate noodles. If you aren't able to buy fresh rice noodles in your local Chinese market, substitute dried ones – but do try the recipe.

METHOD

If you are using dried noodles, soak them in warm water for 20 minutes and drain well before using.

Slice the bitter melon in half lengthwise. Remove the seeds and finely chop the melon. Blanch it in boiling water for 2 minutes and drain thoroughly.

Heat a wok or large frying pan until hot. Add the oil and the garlic and stir-fry for 30 seconds. Put in the pork and stir-fry for 2 minutes, breaking it up. Add the soy sauce, sugar, salt, chicken stock, bitter melon and rice noodles. Continue to stir-fry until the noodles are heated through and most of the liquid has evaporated. Turn onto a platter and serve.

SERVES 4 AS PART OF A CHINESE MEAL, OR 2 AS A SINGLE DISH

1 lb/ 450 g fresh rice noodles or dried, thin rice noodles

1 lb/ 450 g bitter melon

2 tbsp peanut oil

2 tbsp finely chopped garlic

8 oz/ 225 g minced pork

2 tbsp light soy sauce

2 tsp sugar

1 tsp salt

5 fl oz/ 150 ml chicken stock

Fen Xiang Majian Tang He

SWEET SESAME RICE NOODLES

**SERVES 4 AS PART OF A
CHINESE MEAL, OR 2 AS A
SINGLE DISH**

---

1 lb/ 450 g fresh rice
noodles or dried wide,
thin rice noodles

---

4 fl oz/ 125 ml chicken
stock

Sauce

---

5 tbsp sesame paste or
peanut butter

---

3 tbsp sugar

---

5 tbsp warm water

Garnish

---

3 tbsp sugar

A nother Sha He recipe (see p. 91), this unusual sweet dish excited my palate. Redolent of peanuts and sugar, it came as a refreshing counterpoint to some of the salty rice noodle dishes I was served. Although this is not served as a dessert in China, it could easily be enjoyed that way.

METHOD

If using dried noodles, soak them first in warm water for 20 minutes.

Heat the stock in a wok or large frying pan, add the noodles and cook them until they are soft and most of the liquid has evaporated. Turn them out on a warm platter.

While the noodles are cooking, prepare the sauce. In a blender or food processor, mix the sesame paste or peanut butter, sugar and warm water and blend until the sauce is smooth, adding more water if it is too thick. Pour it attractively over the rice noodles, sprinkle with sugar, and serve at once.

Jiuhuang Rousi Chao Mifen

RICE NOODLES WITH YELLOW CHIVES AND PORK

A fter my second visit to our family home, my mother and I left for Hong Kong by a late-afternoon ship. The restaurant at the dock appeared no better or worse than the usual such establishment; that is, the food promised to be dreadful. Much to our surprise, we were served this light and flavorful rice noodle dish, which is perfect for lunch or a light supper. Easy to make, it can be prepared in advance as it reheats very nicely.

METHOD

Soak the dried rice noodles in warm water for 20 minutes. Drain thoroughly.

Cut the pork into thin slices, then stack the slices and finely shred them. In a small bowl, combine the pork with the rice wine or sherry, soy sauce, sesame oil, and cornflour.

Cut the chives or spring onions into 3 in/ 7.5 cm segments.

Heat the wok or frying pan until hot. Add half the oil and the garlic cloves. When the garlic has slightly browned, about 15 seconds, add the pork and stir-fry for 2 minutes. Remove the pork and garlic with a slotted spoon.

Reheat the wok and add the remaining oil. When it is very hot, add the rice noodles, and chives and stir-fry for 30 seconds. Then add the oyster sauce, rice wine or sherry, soy sauces, chicken stock or water, salt and sugar. Continue to stir-fry over medium heat for 5 minutes. Return the pork to the wok or pan and mix well, continuously stir-frying for another minute. Add the sesame oil, turn onto a platter, and serve.

SERVES 4, OR 2 AS A SINGLE DISH

12 oz/ 350 g dried thin rice noodles

8 oz/ 225 g lean pork

1 tsp rice wine or dry sherry

1 tsp light soy sauce

½ tsp sesame oil

½ tsp cornflour

½ lb Chinese yellow or green chives or spring onions

4 tbsp peanut oil

2 peeled garlic cloves, lightly crushed

2 tbsp oyster sauce

1 tbsp rice wine or dry sherry

1 tbsp light soy sauce

1 tbsp dark soy sauce

5 tbsp chicken stock or water

1 tsp salt

1 tsp sugar

1 tbsp sesame oil

Cong Chao Mian

FRIED NOODLE WITH ONIONS

**SERVES 4 AS PART OF A
CHINESE MEAL, OR 2 AS A
SINGLE DISH**

1 lb/ 450 g fresh thin
Chinese egg noodles

8 spring onions, finely
chopped

2 tsp salt

3 tbsp peanut oil

salt to taste

2 tbsp Chinese black
vinegar

P erhaps because I've enjoyed this dish several times during trips to Canton I have managed to reproduce it rather effectively. The noodles are easy to cook and make a wonderful accompaniment or a splendid finale to any meal.

METHOD

Blanch the noodles in a large pot of salted boiling water for 3 minutes and drain thoroughly. Then scatter the noodles on a baking pan, mix in the chopped spring onions and sprinkle the salt over the top.

Heat a 12 in/ 30 cm frying pan, preferably non-stick, with half the oil. When hot, add the noodles, press down to make the noodles conform to the shape of the pan. Turn the heat to very low, and continue to cook for 10 to 15 minutes (sprinkling a spoonful of water from time to time, if the mixture seems to be drying too much), until the bottom is brown. Flip the noodles over in one piece, add more oil as necessary, and continue cooking them until the other side is brown. Sprinkle the noodles with salt and the black vinegar to taste. Slide onto a serving platter and serve.

Rousi Chuan Mian

PORK AND PRESERVED VEGETABLE NOODLE SOUP

E very region in China is chauvinistic about its version of pork and vegetable noodle soup. Sichuan prefers to use preserved vegetables with chilies; in the north, red-in-snow cabbage, another style of preserved vegetables, is used. Whatever the variation, it is a dish common to many food stalls. Once the pork and vegetables are stir-fried, it is a simple matter to place them on the blanched noodles, then to quickly ladle clear broth over all. Of the many versions I have tasted throughout China, I prefer the Sichuan version for lunch or a light supper dish.

METHOD

In a medium-sized bowl, combine the minced pork with the rice wine or sherry, soy sauces, and sesame oil and set aside.

Rinse the Sichuan preserved vegetables in cold running water and finely chop.

Blanch the noodles in a large pot of boiling water for 3 to 5 minutes. Drain the noodles and set aside.

In a large pot, bring the stock to a simmer.

Heat a wok or large frying pan until hot. Add the oil, garlic and ginger, and stir-fry for 10 seconds. Then add the minced pork and preserved vegetables. Stir-fry for 3 minutes, then add the chili bean sauce, chili powder, and sugar. Continue to stir-fry for 2 minutes, mixing well.

Place the noodles in a large bowl or in individual bowls. Add the contents of the wok or pan and then ladle over the soup. Garnish with the spring onions and serve at once.

SERVES 4 AS PART OF A CHINESE MEAL, OR 2 AS A SINGLE DISH

1 lb/ 450 g minced pork

2 tsp rice wine or dry sherry

2 tsp light soy sauce

2 tsp dark soy sauce

1 tsp sesame oil

4 oz/ 125 g Sichuan preserved vegetables

1 lb/ 450 g fresh Chinese noodles

1 ½ pints/ 850 ml chicken stock

1 ½ tbsp peanut oil

2 tbsp finely chopped garlic

1 tbsp finely chopped peeled fresh ginger root

2 tsp chili bean sauce

1 tsp chili powder

1 tsp sugar

Garnish

2 tbsp finely chopped spring onions

Wangfujing Leng Mian

TASTY COLD NOODLES

1 lb/ 450 g fresh or dried
Chinese egg noodles

1 tbsp sesame oil

1 lb/ 450 g cucumbers

6 oz/ 175 g fresh bean
sprouts

Sauce

1 tbsp finely chopped
garlic

1 tbsp finely chopped
peeled fresh ginger root

2 tsp light soy sauce

1 tbsp dark soy sauce

1 tbsp sugar

2 ½ tbsp sesame paste
or peanut butter

1 tbsp sesame oil

1 tbsp white rice vinegar

2 tsp chili oil

2 tbsp granulated sugar

A mong the freshest culinary delights in Beijing today are the privately owned night markets, food stalls located in busy sections throughout the capital. The markets are a little like sidewalk cafes, but without tables and chairs. People sample dishes standing up or walking along. The night markets offer far better food than most of the state-owned eating establishments. Among my favorites is one near Wangfujing (the name derives from a fifteenth-century well), the major shopping area in the capital. It was there I enjoyed this recipe, a delicious platter of noodles, perhaps inspired by Sichuan cooking, that contrasted with the refreshing cucumbers just then in season.

METHOD

If you are using fresh noodles, boil them for 3 to 5 minutes, then drain thoroughly, rinse in cold water and toss immediately in sesame oil. If you are using dried noodles, cook them according to the package instructions or boil for 4 minutes, drain thoroughly, rinse in cold water and toss them in sesame oil.

Peel and slice the cucumbers in half lengthways, and, using a teaspoon, remove the seeds. Cut the cucumber halves into fine long shreds. Rinse the bean sprouts and drain thoroughly.

Mix the sauce ingredients together in a bowl or in a blender. When you are ready to serve, toss the noodles with the sauce, cucumbers, and bean sprouts. Sprinkle with sugar and serve at once.

Guoqiao Mixian

ACROSS THE BRIDGE RICE NOODLES

T his substantial Yunnan soup of rich chicken stock is served scalding hot, with numerous side dishes of chicken and pork, sliced wafer thin, vegetables in season, fresh rice noodles and dipping condiments. All are put into the stock and cooked to perfection at the table. Needless to say, it is vital to serve the stock very hot.

METHOD

Remove the chicken and pork from the freezer and let them sit at room temperature for 30 minutes. Cut them into the thinnest slices possible with a sharp cleaver or knife and arrange them on a platter.

Place the bean sprouts, mushrooms, and rice noodles on another platter. If you are using dried rice noodles, soak them for 15 minutes in hot water and drain thoroughly.

Cut the onions into 2 in/ 5 cm diagonal segments and put into a small bowl. Arrange the condiments on small dishes.

Heat the oven to No 1/ 275°F/ 140°F and put in four large, heat-proof soup bowls. Leave them in the oven for 15 minutes.

Bring the chicken stock to a boil in a medium-sized saucepan. Turn the heat down and keep just simmering. Remove the bowls carefully from the hot oven. Pour in the hot stock. Place all the meat, vegetables, and condiments in the cnter of the table. Let each diner cook the meats, the vegetables, and finally the noodles in the hot stock.

SERVES 4 AS PART OF A CHINESE MEAL, OR 2 AS A SINGLE DISH

6 oz/ 175 g boneless chicken breast, frozen

4 oz/ 125 g boneless lean pork, frozen

4 oz/ 125 g fresh bean sprouts, rinsed

1 oz/ 25 g Chinese dried black mushrooms, soaked, stems removed

1 lb/ 450 g fresh rice noodles or dried rice noodles

4 spring onions

1 ½ pints/ 850 ml rich chicken stock

Dipping condiments

5 tbsp finely chopped spring onions

3 tbsp chili bean sauce

2 tbsp salt mixed with 1 tsp freshly ground black pepper

5 tbsp dark soy sauce

Chao Liangyu Zhusun Mian

NOODLE SOUP WITH CATFISH AND BAMBOO SHOOTS

SERVES 4 AS PART OF A CHINESE MEAL, OR 2 AS A SINGLE DISH

1 lb/ 450 g fresh catfish fillets or any firm, white-fleshed fish fillets such as cod, halibut, haddock, scrod or red snapper, or sole

2 tsp salt

1 egg, beaten

2 tsp cornflour

1 oz/ 25 g Chinese dried black mushrooms

1 lb/ 450 g fresh Chinese noodles

1 ½ pints/ 850 ml chicken stock

3 tbsp peanut oil

1 ½ tbsp peanut oil

2 tbsp finely chopped spring onions

1 tbsp finely chopped peeled fresh ginger root

4 oz/ 125 g bamboo shoots, finely shredded

2 tbsp dried rice wine or dry sherry

F ish provides much of the animal protein in the traditional Chinese diet. Whenever possible, a family or certainly a cooperative farm will have its own fish pond. One evening in Hangzhou, I particularly enjoyed this hot soup of catfish with bamboo shoots in a sauce over noodles. It is a standard item in food stalls: the chicken broth is already prepared, the noodles are ready for blanching, and the fish is quickly stir-fried.

Catfish has a sweet delicate taste. It is bony but lends itself to stir-frying and braising. The texture is slightly flaky when cooked. If catfish fillets are unavailable, substitute any white fish fillets. With a vegetable or salad and some rice, this will make a substantial meal.

METHOD

Cut the catfish or fish fillets into 3 × 1 in/7.5 cm × 25 mm strips and combine with the salt and egg. Sprinkle the strips evenly with the cornflour and set aside.

Soak the mushrooms in warm water for 20 minutes or until they are soft. Rinse under running water to remove any remaining sand. With a sharp knife, remove the stems and discard. Finely shred the mushroom caps.

Blanch the noodles in a pot of boiling water for 2 minutes. Drain thoroughly and set aside.

In a large pot, bring the stock to a simmer.

Heat a wok or large frying pan until hot. Add the oil, and when it is hot pan-fry the fish until it is golden brown. Remove the strips and drain on kitchen paper. Pour out the oil, wipe the wok or pan clean, and reheat. Add the 1 ½ tablespoons of oil, onions and ginger and stir-fry for 15 seconds. Then add the mushrooms, bamboo shoots, rice wine or sherry, soy sauce, sugar and salt. Mix the ingredients together well, and stir-fry for another minute. Return the fish to the wok and combine well.

Place the noodles in a very large bowl, add the stock and the fish, and drizzle the sesame oil over the top. Serve at once.

Huntun Mian

WONTON NOODLE SOUP

SERVES 4 AS PART OF A CHINESE MEAL, OR 2 AS A SINGLE DISH. MAKES 25 WONTONS

Filling

4 oz/ 125 g fatty minced pork

4 oz/ 125 g raw prawns, peeled, deveined, and coarsely chopped

1 tsp rice wine or dry sherry

2 tsp light soy sauce

½ tsp salt

freshly ground black pepper to taste

1 tsp sesame oil

1 package thin square wanton wrappers

8 oz/ 225 g fresh thin wheat or egg noodles

1 ½ pints/ 850 ml chicken stock

salt

Garnish

3 tbsp finely chopped spring onions

The taste of China comes through most clearly in the simplest dishes, and nowhere more clearly than in foods which rely heavily upon classic rich chicken stock, as does this simple recipe. Wonton dumplings and noodles are at their best in this context. Small wonder it is a popular item at fast food stalls throughout southern China where people eat it at all hours of the day or night.

There are probably as many variations on the basic theme of this recipe as there are cooks. Noodle soups outside of Guangdong tend to be a bit heavier than this Cantonese version, which relies upon good, light, clear, rich chicken broth. The thin wheat noodles supply a firm texture to the soup.

METHOD

Mix the filling ingredients together in a medium-sized bowl. Place 2 teaspoons of filling in the center of a wonton square. Pull up the sides and pinch them together to seal. The moisture from the filling should be enough to seal the wontons.

Bring a large pot of water to a boil and blanch the wontons for 3 minutes, drain well, and set aside. Then blanch the noodles for 3 to 5 minutes and drain well.

Bring the stock to a simmer, and season if necessary with salt. Add the noodles and wontons, and simmer for 1 minute. Garnish the soup with the spring onions and serve at once.

Shuijiao

DUMPLINGS IN SOUP

hese popular snacks are also called "warm dumplings" because they float in a wonderfully clear broth. I have enjoyed them in all parts of China, but my favorites are to be found in the street stalls of Guangzhou where the cooks make them just right every time. Fine quality, thin pastry wrappers and a good filling are essential, but a good rich, clear chicken stock is also a basic requirement. Use thin round wrappers for these dumplings, if available. Otherwise use square wonton wrappers. This dash could serve as a soup course or as a substantial snack.

METHOD

Soak the mushrooms in warm water for 20 minutes or until they are soft. Rinse under running water to remove any remaining sand. With a sharp knife, remove the stems and discard. Finely chop the caps and spring onions and coarsely chop the prawns. Combine the chopped mushrooms with the rest of the filling ingredients in a medium-sized bowl.

Place 2 teaspoons of filling in the center of a wonton round. Fold over the round into a half-moon shape. If you are using a wonton square, fold over to make a triangle. Pinch the edges together to seal well.

Bring a large pot of water to a boil and blanch the dumplings for 3 minutes. Remove the dumplings, drain well, and set aside.

Bring the stock to a simmer and season with salt if necessary. Add the dumplings, and simmer for 1 minute. Garnish with the onions and serve at once.

SERVES 4 AS PART OF A CHINESE MEAL, OR 2 AS A SINGLE DISH. MAKES 40 TO 50 DUMPLINGS

Filling

1 oz/ 25 g Chinese dried black mushrooms

8 oz/ 225 g fatty minced pork, shoulder

8 oz/ 225 g raw prawns, peeled, deveined

2 tbsp spring onions

2 tsp rice wine or dry sherry

1 tsp light soy sauce

1 ½ tsp sugar

½ tsp salt

freshly ground black pepper to taste

1 tsp sesame oil

1 package round or square wonton wrappers

1 ½ pints/ 850 ml chicken stock

Garnish

3 tbsp finely chopped spring onions

BEAN CURD AND EGG DISHES

Jing Shao Doufu

BROWN SAUCE DOUFU

T he soft texture of fresh bean curd is delightful to the palate, like chilled freshly baked custard. After braising it briefly in the sauce below, the bean curd takes on a brown color and a quite delicious flavor. Serve the dish with rice.

METHOD

Carefully drain the bean curd and cut it into 2 in/5 cm cubes. Lay the cubes over kitchen paper and continue to drain for another 5 minutes.

Heat a wok or large frying pan until hot. Add the oil, ginger and garlic and stir-fry for 10 seconds. Then add the soy sauce, bean sauces, sugar and sesame oil and stir-fry for another 10 seconds. Now add the cubed bean curd and gently heat it in the sauce, mixing thoroughly. Turn the heat to medium and continue to cook for 5 minutes. Ladle into a serving bowl and serve at once.

SERVES 4 AS PART OF A CHINESE MEAL, OR 2 AS A SINGLE DISH

1 lb/ 450 g fresh soft bean curd

1 ½ tbsp peanut oil

1 tbsp finely chopped peeled fresh ginger root

2 tsp finely chopped garlic

2 tbsp dark soy sauce

1 tbsp yellow bean sauce

1 tsp chili bean sauce

1 tsp sugar

2 tsp sesame oil

Hongshao Doufu

Red-Cooked Bean Curd Family Style

Serves 4 as part of a Chinese meal, or 2 as a single dish

1 lb/ 459 g firm bean curd

8 whole spring onions

4 fl oz/ 125 ml peanut oil

1 ½ tbsp peanut oil

2 tbsp coarsely chopped garlic

2 tbsp rice wine

2 tbsp hoisin sauce

1 tbsp light soy sauce

1 tbsp dark soy sauce

1 tsp sugar

8 fl oz/ 225 ml chicken stock

1 tbsp sesame oil

B ean curd is ideal for braising as it readily absorbs flavors and colors. Chinese bean curd seems to me to be the best in the world, smooth and satiny in texture and invariably perfectly prepared.

Here is a particularly tasty and easy-to-prepare recipe. One of the ingredients, hoisin sauce, adds color and a slightly sweet flavor to the bean curd. The dish reheats nicely.

Method

Cut the bean curd cake into 1 × 3 × 1 in/ 2.5 × 7.5 × 2.5 cm pieces. Lay them on paper towels and drain for another 10 minutes.

At a slight diagonal, cut the spring onions into 3 in/ 7.5 cm pieces.

Heat a wok or frying pan until hot. Add the 125 ml/ 4 fl oz of peanut oil, and when it is hot, fry the bean curd on both sides until it is golden brown. Drain the bean curd well on kitchen paper.

Drain and discard the oil. Wipe the wok or frying pan clean, reheat, and add 1 ½ tablespoons of peanut oil. Then add spring onions and garlic and stir-fry for 30 seconds. Put in the rest of the ingredients except the sesame oil. Bring the mixture to the boil, return the fried bean curd pieces, and cook over high heat for 10 minutes or until the bean curd has absorbed most of the sauce. Add the sesame oil, and give the mixture a final turn. Serve at once.

Doufu Chai

CABBAGE WITH BEAN CURD

SERVES 4 AS PART OF A
CHINESE MEAL, OR 2 AS A
SINGLE DISH

From the Imperial banquet hall to the most humble peasant kitchen, vegetarian dishes have always been included in any special feast. This recipe has been traced to the Long Yin Si Temple in Hangzhou, the ancient capital city of the Southern Song Dynasty (1126–1279 AD). Temple cooking was influenced by Buddhist and Daoist religions, and by the availability of vegetables that lent themselves to subtly sweet but delicious combinations. The extraordinary versatility of bean curd can be seen here in its marriage to the venerable Chinese cabbage.

1 lb firm bean curd

1 lb Chinese cabbage

4 fl oz/ 125 ml peanut oil

1 ½ tbsp peanut oil

3 tbsp finely chopped spring onions

2 tbsp coarsely chopped garlic

2 tbsp rice wine or dry sherry

1 tbsp light soy sauce

½ tsp salt

2 tsp sugar

1 tbsp sesame oil

METHOD

Cut the bean curd into 1 in/ 25 mm squares. Drain well and lay them on kitchen paper to drain for another 10 minutes.

Cut the cabbage into ¼ in/ 6 mm shreds and set aside.

Heat a wok or large frying pan until hot. Add the oil and when it is hot, stir-fry the bean curd on both sides until it is golden brown. Drain well on kitchen paper.

Drain and discard the oil. Wipe the wok or pan clean, reheat, and add the 1 ½ tablespoons of oil. Put in the onions and garlic and stir-fry for 30 seconds. Then add the cabbage and the rest of the ingredients except the sesame oil. Continue to stir-fry for 2 minutes. Return the fried bean curd pieces to the pan and cook over high heat for 5 minutes or until the cabbage has completely cooked. Add the sesame oil and give the mixture a final turn. Serve at once.

Furu Chao Tongcai

CHINESE WATER SPINACH WITH FERMENTED BEAN CURD

SERVES 4 AS PART OF A CHINESE MEAL, OR 2 AS A SINGLE DISH

1 ½–2 lb/ 700–900 g fresh Chinese water spinach or European spinach

2 tbsp peanut oil

3 tbsp chili fermented bean curd or plain fermented bean curd

2 tbsp rice wine or dry sherry

3 tbsp water

Chinese water spinach is a very popular vegetable throughout southern and southwestern China in restaurants and in homes. Chinese water spinach differs from the European variety in that it has hollow stems and arrowhead-shaped leaves. When properly prepared, it offers a nice contrast between the soft leaf and the still-crunchy stem. The fermented bean curd seasoning provides a zesty dimension; this makes a fine accompaniment to any meat dish and is perfect with rice.

METHOD

Wash the Chinese water spinach thoroughly and drain. Cut off 2 in/ 5 cm from the bottom of the stem, which tends to be tough. Cut the rest of the spinach into 4 in/ 10 cm segments.

Heat a wok or large frying pan until hot and add the oil. Put in the fermented bean curd and crush it with a spatula, breaking it into small pieces. Put in the water spinach and stir-fry for 2 minutes. Pour in the rice wine or sherry and water and continue to cook for another 3 minutes. Place on a platter and serve at once.

Ma Po Doufu

GRANDMA CHEN'S BEAN CURD

F oodlore credits Grandma Chen as the creator of many traditional dishes in Sichuan. These are a blend of spicy, peppery, hot, tender, fresh and fragrant ingredients that can be tasted individually and as an ensemble in a kind of food fugue. Take this recipe, for instance. Its essence lies in its seasonings and condiments, their quality, and the care taken in cooking them with the bean curd and beef. This achieves tenderness and contrasting spiciness, while adding garlic at the end of cooking enhances the balance of the whole dish.

METHOD

Gently cut the bean curd into 1 ½ in/ 4 cm cubes.

Heat a wok or large frying pan until hot. Add the oil and beef and stir-fry for 2 minutes to partially cook. Put in the whole yellow bean sauce, soy sauce and salt and continue to stir-fry for another minute. Add the chili powder and continue to stir-fry for 30 seconds. Pour in the stock, add the bean curd and cook for 3 minutes. Stir in the garlic and cornflour mixture and cook for another minute. Ladle the mixture into a serving bowl, garnish with the Sichuan peppercorns, then serve at once.

SERVES 4 AS PART OF A CHINESE MEAL, OR 2 AS A SINGLE DISH

1 lb/ 450 g fresh soft bean curd

2 tbsp peanut oil

8 oz/ 225 g minced beef

2 tbsp whole yellow bean sauce

2 tbsp dark soy sauce

½ tsp salt

2 tsp ground red chili powder

12 fl oz/ 350 ml chicken stock

2 tbsp coarsely chopped garlic

2 tsp cornflour mixed with 1 tbsp water

Garnish

1 tbsp Sichuan peppercorns, roasted and finely ground

Guizhou Lianai Doufu

GUIZHOU-STYLE BEAN CURD

**SERVES 4 AS PART OF
CHINESE MEAL, OR 2 AS A
SINGLE DISH**

1 lb/ 450 g firm bean
curd

16 fl oz/ 450 ml oil, for
deep frying

Filling

1 tbsp peanut oil

3 tbsp finely chopped
fresh coriander

2 tbsp finely chopped
garlic

2 tbsp finely chopped
spring onions

1 ½ tbsp finely chopped
peeled fresh ginger root

1 to 2 tsp red chili flakes
or ½ to 1 tsp ground red
chili powder

1 tbsp dark soy sauce

1 tsp sugar

½ tsp salt

½ tsp sesame oil

The first time I tasted this dish was at a family feast in Yunnan. The firm bean curd was filled with fresh ginger, chili, garlic, fresh coriander, a touch of soy sauce and a local herb called *yu dan cao*. This last ingredient, unavailable in the West, gave a sharp earthy tang; spring onions make an admirable substitute.

Vegetarians will delight in this dish as a main course or it can be served as a side dish with or without meat. It can be prepared in advance, as it reheats nicely. You might want to reduce the chili by half the first time you prepare it. I love very hot foods.

METHOD

Drain the bean curd and cut it into 2 in/ 50 cm squares. Leave them to drain for 10 minutes on paper towels.

Heat a wok or large frying pan until hot. Add the tablespoon of oil and the rest of the filling ingredients and stir-fry for 1 minute. Transfer these ingredients to a bowl and allow them to cool thoroughly.

Heat a wok or large frying pan until hot. Add the oil for deep-frying and when hot, cook the bean curd on both sides until it is golden brown. Remove the bean curd squares from the wok, drain them well on kitchen paper and allow them to cool thoroughly. Discard the oil.

Take each bean curd square and split it open slightly with a knife on one side to form a pocket. Place a spoonful of cooked filling in each of the pockets. Continue to fill the squares until you have used all the bean curd.

Wipe the wok clean, reheat, and add the table-spoon of oil for the sauce. Then add the garlic and ginger and stir-fry for 30 seconds. Then add the rest of the sauce ingredients except the corn-flour mixture and sesame oil. Bring the mixture to a boil, return the fried bean curd pieces to the wok and cook over medium heat for 3 minutes. Add the cornflour mixture, stir gently to com-bine, and then add the sesame oil. Give the mix-ture a final turn and serve at once.

Sauce

1 tbsp peanut oil

1 tbsp finely chopped garlic

1 tbsp finely chopped peeled fresh ginger root

1 tbsp dark soy sauce

1 tbsp rice wine or dry sherry

2 tsp light soy sauce

1 tsp sugar

8 fl oz/ 225 ml chicken stock

1 tsp cornflour mixed with 1 tsp water

2 tsp sesame oil

Jidan Chao Xihongshi

STIR-FRIED EGGS WITH TOMATOES

**SERVES 4 AS PART OF A
CHINESE MEAL, OR 2 AS A
SINGLE DISH**

6 eggs, beaten

2 tsp sesame oil

1 tsp salt

1 lb/ 450 g fresh ripe
tomatoes

6 whole spring onions

1 ½ tbsp peanut oil

½ tsp salt

Whoever travels to the remoter parts of China is guaranteed some surprises. I experienced one in Yunnan province when I visited the tiny village of Yi Liang Gou Jie, a place that even my friends who live in the province had never been to. There I stumbled upon a rustic tea house/restaurant with no sign or nameplate, but someone's goat tethered in front. The speciality of the house was Yunnan duck, several seasonal vegetable dishes, and this delectable stir-fry of eggs and tomatoes. It was quite a repast for the middle of nowhere at the no-name cafe. The delicate flavor of the fresh eggs nicely balances the sweet acidity of the ripe tomatoes.

METHOD

In a medium-sized bowl, combine the eggs with the sesame oil and salt and reserve.

Cut the tomatoes into quarters and then into eighths. With the side of a cleaver or knife, crush the spring onions, then finely shred them.

Heat a wok or large frying pan until hot. Add the oil, salt and onions and stir-fry for 30 seconds. Then add the tomatoes and eggs and continue to cook stirring continually until eggs are set, about 5 minutes. Quickly place on a platter and serve at once.

Jiuwang Chao Dan

STIR-FRIED EGGS WITH YELLOW CHIVES

S tir-fried eggs are a popular food in the countryside: chickens are plentiful and eggs are abundant. Urban dwellers, even in China, rarely get to enjoy these yellow chives, but country dwellers grow their own. A paler version of Chinese green chives, they are sheltered from the sun while growing, blocking the formation of chlorophyll. The chives are delicate and tender, with an earthy taste; they must be cooked immediately after they are picked. You may substitute Chinese green chives or spring onions if necessary, but Western chives have a completely different taste.

METHOD

In a medium-sized bowl, combine the eggs with the sesame oil and ½ teaspoon salt. Set aside. Cut the chives and spring onions on a slight diagonal into 3 in/ 7.5 cm pieces.

Heat a wok or large frying pan until it is hot. Add the oil, salt, chives and spring onions and stir-fry until the chives and spring onions are wilted, about 2 minutes. Then add the eggs and continue to cook until the eggs have just set. Quickly place on a platter and serve at once.

SERVES 3 AS PART OF A CHINESE MEAL, OR 1 AS A SINGLE DISH

4 eggs, beaten

2 tsp sesame oil

½ tsp salt

8 oz/ 225 g Chinese yellow or green chives

4 whole spring onions

1 ½ tbsp peanut oil

½ tsp salt

SOME BASICS OF CHINESE COOKING

AUBERGINE

A popular and inexpensive food found throughout China. These pleasing purple-skinned vegetables range in size from the larger plump ones, easy to find in all produce stores, to the small thin variety which the Chinese prefer for their more delicate flavor. Look for those with smooth unblemished skin.

Chinese cooks normally do not peel aubergines, since the skin preserves texture, taste and shape. Large aubergines should be cut according to the recipe, sprinkled with a little salt, and left to sit for 20 minutes. They should then be rinsed and any liquid blotted dry with kitchen towels. This process extracts bitter juices and the aubergine also absorbs less moisture in the cooking process. This procedure is unnecessary if you are using Chinese aubergines.

BAMBOO SHOOTS

Bamboo shoots are the young edible shoots of certain kinds of bamboo (part of the grass family). There are as many different types of bamboo shoots as there are kinds of bamboo – and at least ten of the hundred or so are marketed. They generally fall into two broad categories: spring shoots and winter shoots, the winter being smaller and more tender than the spring ones, which tend to be quite large. Expensive, fresh bamboo shoots are found only seasonally in markets in China; however, canned ones are available in the West and are more resonably priced. Canned bamboo shoots tend to be pale yellow with a crunchy texture and, in some cases, a slightly sweet flavor. They come peeled and either whole or thickly sliced. Rinse them thoroughly and blanch them for two minutes in boiling water before use. Transfer any remaining shoots to a jar, cover them with fresh water, and refrigerate them. If the water is changed daily they will keep two or three days. Slice blanched bamboo shoots before proceeding with the recipe.

Fresh bamboo shoots are prepared by first stripping off all their leaves and then trimming the hard base. Only the tender center core is edible, which is cut and blanched for at least five minutes to remove its bitterness. The shoots are then ready to be stir-fried or cooked.

BEAN CURD – DOUFU

Bean curd is also known by its Chinese name, doufu, or by its Japanese name, tofu. It has played an important part in Chinese cookery for over a thousand years because it is highly nutritious, rich in protein, and goes well with other foods. Bean curd has a distinctive smooth texture but a bland taste. It is made from yellow soybeans which are soaked, ground, mixed with water and then cooked briefly before being soldified. It is usually sold in two forms: as firm, small blocks or in a soft, custard-like variety, but it is also available in several dried forms and in a fermented version. The soft bean curd (sometimes called silken tofu) is used for soups and other dishes, while the solid type is used for stir-frying, braising, and deep-frying. Solid bean curd blocks are white in color and are packed in water in plastic containers. Once opened, they can be kept in their containers in the refrigerator for up to five days, provided the water is changed daily. To use solid bean curd, carefully cut the amount required into cubes or shreds using a sharp knife, then cook it gently. Too much stirring can cause it to disintegrate, though this does not affect its nutritional value.

FERMENTED BEAN CURD (RED, CHILI, AND REGULAR)

This is a cheese-like form of bean curd preserved in rice or in wine, in brine with rice, or in chilies, and sold in glass jars at Asian speciality markets.

It is very popular in China where it is eaten by itself with rice or used in cooking or as a condiment. It is used as a flavoring agent, especially with vegetables. It comes in several forms: the red fermented bean curd has been cured in a brine with red rice, rice wine, and sometimes with crushed dried chili peppers, and the regular one has been made with wine. Once the jar has been opened, fermented bean curd will keep indefinitely if resealed and refrigerated.

PRESSED SEASONED BEAN CURD

When water is extracted from fresh bean curd cakes by pressing them with a weight, the bean curd becomes firm and compact. Simmered in water with soy sauce, star anise, and sugar, the pressed bean curd acquires a smooth, resilient texture that is quite unusual. Cut into small pieces, it can be stir-fried with meat or vegetables; when cut into larger pieces it can be simmered. Buy it at Asian speciality markets, or substitute fresh firm bean curd.

BEAN SPROUTS

Now widely available, these are the sprouts of the green mung bean, although some Chinese markets also stock yellow soybean sprouts which are much larger. Chinese markets also stock yellow soybean sprouts which are much larger. Bean sprouts should always be very fresh and crunchy. They will keep for several days loosely wrapped in kitchen paper and inside a plastic bag stored in the vegetable crisper of a refrigerator.

BIRD'S NEST

A truly exotic food, and one of the most sought-after delicacies of China. Historically, it was most abundant in southern China, and is now sought after in affluent Hong Kong and Taiwan. This is literally bird's nest made of regurgitated spittle of a certain type of swift from the East Asian tropics: Thailand, Vietnam, Java, and the Philippines.

Their nests are found in large mountainside caverns where workers climb on long bamboo scaffolding to retrieve them. Bird's nest is said to be good for one's complexion and is prescribed for convalescing patients. It is sold dried and must be soaked before using, as instructed in recipes calling for it. The result, like shark's fin, is a bland, soft, crunchy jelly that relies for flavor on whatever sauce or broth it is served with. It is an acquired taste.

BITTER MELON

This unusual vegetable is also an acquired taste that has as many detractors as it has fans. Bitter melon has a bumpy dark to pale green skin, and has a slightly bitter quinine flavor that has a cooling effect in one's mouth. In some parts of China it is often dried and used as medicine. The greener the melon, the more bitter its taste, and many cooks look for the milder yellow-green varieties. To use, cut in half, seed, and discard interior membrane. Then, to lessen its bitter taste, either blanch or salt in, according to instructions in your recipe. Store in the bottom of your refrigerator in a loose plastic or paper bag. It should keep there for three to five days, depending on the condition in which it was bought.

BLACK BEANS

These small black soybeans, also known as salted black beans or fermented black beans, are preserved by being fermented with salt and spices. They have a distinctive, slightly salty taste and a pleasantly rich smell, and are used as a seasoning, often in conjunction with garlic or fresh ginger root. Together, they are among the most popular flavors of southern China. They are easy to find in the West and I see them often in supermarkets. You can find them in cans marked "Black Bean Sauce", but I prefer those packed in plastic bags. Although some recipes say to rinse them before using, I notice that most chefs in China do not bother with this. The beans will keep indefinitely if stored in the refrigerator or in a cool place.

CAUL FAT

Actually the lower stomach lining of a pig or cow, this lacy membrane melts during cooking and keeps meats and fillings moist and delicious. It is highly perishable so buy it in small quantities and use quickly. For longer storage, wrap the caul fat carefully and freeze. To defrost, rinse in cold water. I find that soaking layers of caul fat in cold water helps to separate them without tearing its fragile webs. You can order caul fat from your local butcher.

CHILIES, FRESH

Fresh chilies – the seed pods of the capsicum plant – are used extensively and are popular in Chinese cuisine. However, the type of chili most often found is not as pungent or spicy as the ones found in many parts of southeast Asia and parts of the United States. Although relatively new to Chinese cuisine, as it comes from the Americas, the chili has spread rapidly throughout Asia. In China, fresh chilies are small to medium size, and generally red, but they also come in shades of green. Smaller varieties can be found, but the larger, longer ones are the ones most available; their taste is mildly spicy and pungent.

Throughout the recipes, I have used the mildest variety I can find, cutting down the amounts to compensate for the slightly hotter varieties found in the West. Look for fresh chilies that are bright, with no brown patches or black spots. Use red chilies wherever possible, as they are generally milder than green ones because they sweeten as they ripen.

To prepare fresh chilies, first rinse them in cold water. Then, using a small, sharp knife, slit them lengthways. Remove and discard the seeds. Rinse the chilies well under cold running water, then prepare them according to the instructions in the recipe. Wash your hands, knife, and chopping board before preparing other foods or touching your eyes.

CHILIES, DRIED RED

A beautiful sight in food shops, at the front of restaurants and in the homes of Sichuan are the long strings of dried red chilies. Used less frequently in other areas of China, they are essential to many Sichuan-inspired dishes. They are used in either whole or ground form. Some are small and thin, ½–1 in/ 12.25 mm long. They are used to season oil for stir-fried dishes, or split and chopped and used in sauces and for braising. They are normally left whole, cut in half lengthways, or finely ground with the seeds left in. Dried chilies will keep indefinitely in a tightly covered jar in a cool place.

CHILI OIL/CHILI DIPPING SAUCE

Chili oil is sometimes used as a dipping condiment as well as a seasoning in China, where it is generally milder than the commercially made chili oil from Sichuan Province, and certainly never as hot as the oil from Southeast Asia. The Thai and Malaysian versions are especially hot.

You can purchase chili oil from Chinese markets. Commercial products are quite acceptable, but I include this recipe because the homemade version is the best. Remember that chili oil is too dramatic to be used as the sole cooking oil; it should be combined with milder oils, or with other flavors for a dipping sauce or condiment. I include Sichuan pepper and black beans.

Once made, chili oil will keep for months if it is stored in a tightly sealed glass jar and kept in a cool, dark place.

6 fl oz/ 175 ml peanut oil
2 tbsp chopped dried red chilies
1 tbsp whole unroasted Sichuan peppercorns
2 tbsp whole black beans

Heat a wok over a high heat and add the oil and the rest of the ingredients. Continue to cook over a low heat for about 10 minutes. Allow the mixture to cool undisturbed and then pour it into a jar. Let the mixture sit for 2 days, and then strain the oil.

CHILI BEAN SAUCE   See Sauces and Pastes, p. 138.

CHILI POWDER   Chili powder, made from dried red chilies, is pungent and aromatic, ranging from hot to very hot, and widely used in many spicy dishes. In Sichuan, it is often combined with ground roasted Sichuan peppercorns.

CHINESE BROCCOLI   Chinese broccoli is not like European-type broccoli. It is very crunchy and slightly bitter and more resembles Swiss chard in flavor. It is quite delicious with an earthy, "green" taste. It has deep olive green leaves and sometimes white flowers. It is usually only available at Chinese markets. Look for stems which are firm and leaves which look fresh and green. It is prepared in exactly the same way as broccoli and should be stored in a plastic bag in the vegetable crisper of the refrigerator where it will keep for several days. Where Chinese broccoli is not available, substitute ordinary broccoli.

CHINESE CHIVES   Chinese chives, widely used in China, are related to common chives and are of the garlic family. They have an earthy, oniony taste, stronger and more garlic-like than our chives, and their flowers can be used as well as the blades. Chinese chives can be found in Chinese markets but they are easily grown in home herb gardens. Look for wide flat blades and sprays of white, star-shaped flowers. They can be substituted for regular chives but adjust the quantity to allow for their stronger flavor. Rinse and dry the chives, store them in a slightly damp kitchen paper inside a plastic bag in the refrigerator and use as soon as possible.

Chinese yellow chives are Chinese chives which have been grown in the dark and are therefore pale yellow in color – like Chicory – and have a more subtle flavor than the green Chinese chives.

CHINESE FLOWERING CABBAGE

Chinese flowering cabbage is part of the large mustard green cabbage family and is found frequently in dishes in China, especially in the south, where it is usually known by the more familiar Cantonese name, *choi sum*. Chinese flowering cabbage has green leaves and may have small yellow flowers which are eaten along with the leaves and stems. It is delicious stir-fried.

CHINESE CABBAGE

Chinese cabbage, also popularly known as Peking cabbage, comes fresh in various sizes from long, compact and bullet-shaped to fat and squat-looking. All types are tightly packed with firm, pale green (or in some cases slightly yellow), crinkled leaves. This versatile vegetable is used for soups or it is stir-fried with meats, absorbing flavors easily because of its sponge-like quality. Used raw or lightly cooked, the cabbage has mild, sweet flavor which complements richer foods.

CHINESE LONG BEANS

These beans are popular in China and can be found in great abundance in the markets there. They are also known as yard-long beans and can grow to 3 ft/ 91.5 cm in length. Not related to short, Western green beans, long beans originated in Asia. There are two varieties: the pale green ones and the dark green, thinner ones. Buy those that are fresh and bright green, with no dark marks. You will usually find long beans sold in looped bunches, and there is no need to string them before cooking. In China, they are stir-fried with meats or with fermented bean curd. They have a crunchy taste and texture like string beans but cook faster.

Store the fresh beans in a plastic bag in the refrigerator and use within four days.

CHINESE MUSHROOMS, DRIED

There are many grades of these wonderful mushrooms said to have been cultivated for more than a thousand years in southern China. Black or brown, the best are very large ones with a lighter color and a highly cracked surface; these are usually the most expensive. Chinese markets specializing in dried food carry all grades heaped in mounds, with the most expensive mushrooms elaborately boxed, sometimes in plastic. Fresh mushrooms (popularly known by their Japanese name, Shiitake) are not an adequate substitute and the Chinese almost never use them fresh, preferring the dried version's distinct, robust, smoky flavors, and the way they absorb sauces, taking on a succulent texture. They are used as seasonings, finely chopped and combined with meats, fish, and shellfish. Keep them stored in an airtight jar in a cool, dry place.

TO USE CHINESE DRIED MUSHROOMS

Soak the mushrooms in a bowl of warm water for about 20 minutes or until they are soft and pliable. Squeeze out the excess water and cut off and discard the woody stems. Only the caps are used.

Strain the soaking water through a fine sieve to remove any sand or residue from the dried mushrooms and save it to use in soups and in water for cooking rice.

CHINESE TREE FUNGUS

These tiny, black, dried leaves are also known as cloud ears; when soaked, they puff up to look like little clouds. Soak the dried fungus in hot water for 20 to 30 minutes until soft. Rinse well, cutting away any hard portions. Fungi are valued for their crunchy texture and slightly smoky flavor. You can find them at Chinese markets, usually wrapped in plastic or cellophane bags. They keep indefinitely in a jar stored in a cool, dry place.

The larger variety of the Chinese tree fungi described above. Prepare, soak, and trim them in the same manner. Once soaked, they will swell up to four or five times their size. Rinse well and cut away any hard portions. Sold in Chinese markets they keep indefinitely when stored in a cool, dry place.

CHINESE WOOD EAR FUNGUS

Chinese white cabbage, popularly known as bok choy, has been grown in China for centuries. Although there are many varieties, the most common and best known is the one with a long, smooth, milky-white stem and large, crinkly, dark green leaves. The size of the plant indicates how tender it is. The smaller the better, especially in the summer, when the hot weather toughens the stalks. Bok choy has a light, fresh, slightly mustardy taste and requires little cooking. In China, bok choy is used in soup or is stir-fried. Now widely available in supermarkets, look for firm crisp stalks and unblemished leaves. Store bok choy in the vegetable crisper of your refrigerator.

CHINESE WHITE CABBAGE – BOK CHOY

Chinese white radish is also known as Chinese icicle radish, as mooli, or by its Japanese name, daikon. It is long and white and rather like a carrot in shape but usually much larger. A winter radish, it can withstand long cooking without disintegrating and thus absorbs the flavors of the food it is cooked with, yet retains its distinctive radish taste and texture. In China, these root vegetables are usually found in home dishes, treated the way Western cooks use potatoes or carrots. They are never used without being peeled. Look for firm, heavy, solid and unblemished ones. They should be slightly translucent inside, solid and not fibrous. You can find them in some supermarkets and almost always at Chinese or Asian markets. Store in a plastic bag in the vegetable crisper of your refrigerator where they will keep for over a week.

CHINESE WHITE RADISH

**CINNAMON STICKS
OR BARK**

Cinnamon sticks are curled, paper-thin pieces of the bark of the cinnamon tree, the Chinese version being rather thick. They are highly aromatic and more pungent than the common cinnamon sticks, but the latter are an adequate substitute. They add a robust taste to braised dishes and are an important ingredient of five-spice powder. Store cinnamon sticks or bark in a tightly sealed jar to preserve their aroma and flavor. Ground cinnamon is too strong and not a satisfactory substitute.

CITRUS PEEL
(DRIED TANGERINE
PEEL, DRIED
ORANGE PEEL)

In the markets of China you will often find freshly peeled greenish lemons with the fruit sold separately from the peel. Many people take the peels home and dry them to use in fish or meat dishes. The best citrus peels are those of Chinese tangerines, which have a rich, slightly sweet orange flavor. Dried citrus peel is sold in Asian or Chinese grocery stores or can be easily made at home. Wash and rinse the fruit well. Cut each fruit into eight wedges. Use a sharp knife to cut off the fruit sections and then carefully separate the white pith from the peel. Dry the peel on a rack in a warm place until it is hard. Stored in an air-tight jar, the dried peel will last for months. When you are ready to use the peel, rehydrate it in a bowl of warm water for 20 minutes or until it is soft.

**CORIANDER –
CHINESE PARSLEY
– CILANTRO**

Fresh coriander is one of the relatively few herbs used in Chinese cookery and is a standard in southern China. It looks like flat parsley but its pungent, musky, citrus-like character gives it an unmistakable flavor. Its feathery leaves are often used as a garnish, or it is chopped and then mixed into sauces and stuffings. When buying fresh coriander, look for deep green, fresh-looking leaves.

To store coriander, wash it in cold water, drain it thoroughly or spin dry in a salad spinner and put it in a clean plastic bag along with a couple of sheets of moist kitchen towel.

CORNFLOUR

In China and throughout Asia there are many flours and types of starch, such as water chestnut powder, taro starch, and arrowroot, which are used to bind and thicken sauces and to make batter. Cornflour is also now widely used in Chinese cooking, although traditional cooks prefer a bean flour because it thickens faster and holds longer. In China, sauces are light and barely coat the food, and food never "swims" in thick sauces. As part of a marinade, cornflour helps to coat food properly and to give dishes a velvety texture. It also protects food during deep-frying by helping to seal in the juices, producing a crisper coating than flour, and can be used as a binder for minced stuffings. Cornflour is invariably blended with cold water until it forms a smooth paste and added at the last moment to sauces. The mixture will look milky at first, but when the dish is properly prepared, the cornflour turns clear and shiny as it thickens the sauce.

DRIED SHRIMPS

Dried shrimps are used to perk up fried rice or mixed with meat dishes to give an added dimension. Tiny dried shrimps are sold in packages and may be found in Asian speciality markets. Look for the brands with the pinkest color and avoid grayish ones. Dried shrimps will keep indefinitely sealed in a glass container and stored in a cool, dry place. When cooked, the dried shrimps add a delicate taste to sauces; cooking moderates the shrimps' strong odor.

EGG WHITE

Egg whites are often used in Chinese recipes as ingredients of batters and coatings, sealing in flavor and juices and making a light and protective coating for foods when plunged into warm oil, especially for velveting. One egg white from a large egg generally measures about 2 tablespoons. Egg whites freeze well in tablespoon-size cubes in an ice tray.

FIVE-SPICE POWDER

Less commonly known as five-flavored powder or five-fragrance spice powder, this brownish powder is a mixture of star anise, Sichuan peppercorns, fennel, cloves, and cinnamon. A good blend is pungent, fragrant, spicy and slightly sweet at the same time. You can find it in the spice section of good supermarkets or Asian speciality markets.

FLOUR

RICE FLOUR

This flour is made from raw rice and is used to make fresh rice noodles. Store it as you would wheat flour.

GLUTINOUS RICE FLOUR

This flour, made from glutinous rice, gives a chewy texture to the dough and is widely used in China for making rich dim sum pastries. However, it is not an acceptable substitute in recipes that call for regular rice flour, but can be stored in the same way.

GARLIC

The pungent flavor of garlic is part of the fabric of China's cuisine, and it would be inconceivable to cook without this distinctive, highly aromatic smell and taste. It is used in numerous ways: whole, finely chopped, crushed, and pickled. In China I have even found it smoked. It is used to flavor oils as well as spicy sauces, and is often paired with other equally pungent ingredients such as scallions, black beans, curry, shrimp paste or fresh ginger. In China, cooks often add a smashed clove of garlic to the hot oil. The garlic becomes fragrant and is said to have "sweetened" the oil; it is then removed and discarded.

Select fresh garlic which is firm and heavy, the cloves preferably pinkish in color. It should be stored in a cool, dry place, but not in the refrigerator where it can easily become mildewed or begin sprouting.

GARLIC SHOOTS

These are young garlic shoots before they begin to form a bulb. Harvested early in the spring, they are mild and delicately perfumed. They look a bit like spring onions their green tops may also be used as a garnish or flavoring.

GINGER ROOT

In traditional Chinese cooking fresh ginger root is as essential as the wok. It is said that ginger root from Canton is the most aromatic, but, like garlic, it is an indispensable ingredient of all Chinese cookery. Pungent, spicy, and fresh in flavour, these rhizomes are a golden-beige color with a thin dry skin. They range from small, broken-off bits to large knobby "hands". In China you can find peeled ginger root at the markets; older, more shriveled ginger root is used for medicinal broths. Look for ginger root which is firm, solid, and clear-skinned.

Young stem ginger often makes a seasonal appearance in the markets of China, but is hard to find in the West. So tender it does not need peeling, fresh young ginger can be eaten on its own as a vegetable. It is also commonly pickled in China.

Ginger root wrapped in plastic will keep in the refrigerator for up to two weeks. Peeled ginger root covered in rice wine or dry sherry in a jar and refrigerated will last for several months. This has the added benefit of producing a flavored wine.

GINGER JUICE

Made from fresh ginger, the juice is used in marinades to give a subtle ginger taste without the pungency of the fresh chopped pieces. Here is a simple method of extracting the juice: cut fresh unpeeled ginger root into 1 in/ 25 mm chunks and drop them into a running food processor. When the ginger is finely chopped, squeeze out the juice by hand through a cotton or linen towel. Or, mash the ginger with a kitchen mallet or the side of a cleaver or knife until most of the fibers are exposed. Then simply squeeze out the juice by hand through a cotton or linen towel.

LEEKS

This vegetable is grown and used primarily in northern China. It is treated as an onion and stir-fried with meats. The leeks found in China are large, cylindrical and resemble a giant spring onion with a white husk, like garlic. Leeks found in the West are a good substitute.

LILY BUDS

Also known as tiger lily buds, golden needles or lily stems, dried lily buds are an ingredient in *muxi* (*mu shu*) dishes and hot and sour soups. They provide texture as well as an earthy taste to any dish. Soak the buds in hot water for about 30 minutes or until soft. Cut off the hard ends and shred or cut in half according to the recipe directions. You can find them in Chinese markets; they are quite inexpensive. Store them in a jar in a dry place.

MALTOSE SUGAR

See also Sugar, p. 143
This type of malt sugar is a liquid syrup that adds a wonderful richness to stews and sauces without a cloying sweetness. It may be stored at room temperature and is only found in Chinese markets. Honey may be used as a substitute.

NOODLES

In China, people eat noodles of all kinds, day and night, in restaurants and at food stalls. Several styles of Chinese noodle dishes have now made their way to the West, including the fresh thin egg noodles which are browned (cooked) on both sides and the popular thin rice noodles. Both kinds can be bought in Chinese markets fresh and dried. Below is a list of the major types of noodles.

WHEAT NOODLES AND EGG NOODLES

These are made from hard or soft wheat flour and water. If egg has been added the noodles are usually labeled as egg noodles. Flat noodles are usually used in soups and round noodles are best for stir-frying or pan-frying. The fresh ones freeze nicely if they are well wrapped. Thaw them thoroughly before cooking. Noodles are very good cooked and served with main dishes instead of plain rice. I think dried wheat or fresh egg noodles are best for this.

TO COOK WHEAT AND EGG NOODLES

If you are using fresh noodles, immerse them in a pot of boiling water and cook them for 3 to 5 minutes or until you like their texture. If you are using dried noodles, either cook them according to the instructions on the packet, or cook them in boiling water for 4 to 5 minutes. Drain and serve.

If you are cooking noodles ahead of time or before stir-frying them, toss the cooked and drained noodles in 2 tsp of sesame oil and put them into a bowl. Cover this with plastic wrap and refrigerate for up to 2 hours.

RICE NOODLES

Rice noodles are popular in southern China, where they are widely known as Sha He noodles, the name deriving from a small village outside the city of Guangzhou (Canton). The fresh ones are called "fen noodles", and are prepared in a different manner (see Fen Noodles). The dried noodles are opaque white and come in a variety of shapes. One of the most common examples is rice stick noodles, which are flat and about the length of a chopstick. They can also vary in thickness. Use the type called for in the recipes. Rice noodles are very easy to use. Simply soak them in water for 20 minutes until they are soft. Drain them in a colander or a sieve and they are then ready to be used in soups or to be stir-fried.

FEN RICE NOODLES (ALSO KNOWN AS SHA HE NOODLES)

The Chinese make large sheets of *fen*, which means rice noodles, from a basic mixture of rice flour, wheat *starch* (not flour), and water. This pasta is steamed in sheets and then, when cooked, is cut into noodles to be eaten immediately, most often served with a sauce.

BEAN THREAD
(TRANSPARENT)
NOODLES

These noodles, also called cellophane noodles, are made from ground mung beans and not from a grain flour. Freshly made ones can sometimes be seen in China, fluttering in the breeze on lines like drying clothes. They are available dried, and are very fine and white. Easy to recognize, packed in their neat, plastic-wrapped bundles, they are stocked by most Chinese markets and some supermarkets. They are never served on their own, but are added to soups or braised dishes or are deep-fried and used as a garnish. They must be soaked in warm water for about 5 minutes before use. As they are rather long you might find it easier to cut them into shorter lengths after soaking. If you are frying them, they do not need soaking beforehand but do need to be separated. A good technique for separating the strands is to pull them apart while holding them in a large paper bag which stops them from flying all over the place.

OILS

Oil is the most commonly used cooking medium in China. While animal fats, usually lard and chicken fat, are used in some regions, particularly in northern parts of China, the oil of choice is peanut. It is also the most expensive.

CORN OIL

A healthful, mostly polyunsaturated oil that is good for cooking and also has a high burning point. I use corn oil in a pinch but find it rather heavy and am always aware of the distinctive smell and taste. It is used in China, but it is not as popular as vegetable or peanut oil.

OTHER VEGETABLE
OILS

Some of the cheaper vegetable oils are available in China: these include rapeseed, cottonseed, soybean, safflower, and sunflower oils. They are light in color and taste and can be used in cooking, although they tend to smoke rather quickly. In China, they are used mainly by food stalls and the cheaper restaurants. They are quite edible but simply not as good nor as efficient as peanut oil.

PEANUT OIL

The Chinese prefer to cook with peanut oil because it has a pleasant, mild, unobtrusive taste. It can be heated to a high temperature without burning and this makes it perfect for stir-frying and deep-frying. The peanut oils found in China are cold pressed and have the fragrance of freshly roasted peanuts. Some Chinese supermarkets stock the Chinese brands, their names written in Chinese characters. These are well worth the search, but if you cannot find them, use a peanut oil from your local supermarket.

SESAME OIL

This aromatic and strongly flavored, thick, rich, golden brown or dark colored oil is made from toasted and roasted sesame seeds, which have a distinctive, nutty flavor and aroma. It is widely used in China, although in limited amounts and not normally for cooking. Only in northern China do cooks sometimes combine it with other oils as a cooking oil. Added as a final seasoning, or used as a marinade, it subtly enriches a dish without overcoming its basic flavor.

OYSTERS, DRIED

Like many dried seafood found in China, these oysters are frequently used in finely minced form to enhance dishes, but use them carefully because they can overwhelm a dish with their assertive flavors. Soak them until soft for at least one hour in a bowl of warm water, or even as long as overnight. If you wish, you may substitute canned smoked oysters.

PEANUTS

Raw peanuts are used to add flavor and a crunchy texture and are especially popular in China. They are stir-fried before being added to dishes. The thin red skins need to be removed before you use the nuts. To do this, simply immerse them in a pot of boiling water for about 2 minutes. Drain them and let them cool, and the skins will come off easily.

RED-IN-SNOW CABBAGE

This hardy winter vegetable peeks through the snow with red or crimson colors, thus its name. The cabbage is pickled and can be bought in cans at Asian speciality markets. It adds a pungent, slightly sour taste to dishes when used as a flavoring, or it can be used as an interestingly textured vegetable ingredient in stir-fried dishes.

RICE
LONG-GRAIN RICE

This is the most popular rice for cooking in China where there are many different varieties. Although the Chinese go through the ritual of washing it, rice purchased at supermarkets doesn't require this step.

SHORT-GRAIN RICE

Most frequently found in northern China and used for making rice porridge, a popular morning meal. I find it to be coarse and rough.

GLUTINOUS RICE

Also known as sweet rice or sticky rice. It is short, round and pearl-like, with a higher gluten content, and is used in China for stuffings, rice pudding, and in pastries. It is used for rice dishes, sometimes wrapped in lotus leaves, and served after Chinese banquets. It is also used for making Chinese rice wine and vinegar. Most Chinese markets and some supermarkets stock it. Glutinous rice must be soaked for at least 2 hours (preferably overnight) and cooked in the same way as long-grain rice.

TO WASH RICE

An optional step, if you wish to do as the Chinese do. Put the required amount of rice into a large bowl. Fill the bowl with cold water and swish the rice around with your hands. Carefully pour off the cloudy water, keeping the rice in the bowl. Repeat this process several times until the water is clear.

An important component to the flavors of China. This wine is used extensively for cooking and drinking throughout all of China, but I believe the finest of its many varieties to be from Shaoxing in Zhejiang Province in eastern China. It is made from glutinous rice, yeast and spring water. Now readily available in the West from Chinese markets and some wine shops, it should be kept tightly corked at room temperature. Do not confuse this wine with sake, which is the Japanese version of rice wine and quite different. A good quality, dry pale sherry can be substituted but cannot equal its rich, mellow taste. Other Western grape wines are not an adequate substitute.

RICE WINE

Table salt is the finest grind of salt. Many chefs feel that kosher or sea salt has a richer flavor than ordinary table salt. Sea salt is frequently found in bins at the Chinese markets. Rock salt is most often known for its role in freezing ice cream, but the larger crystals make an excellent medium of heat conduction, and rock salt is often used in certain kinds of Chaozhou (a regional southern cooking style), especially with chicken or squab dishes.

SALT (KOSHER, ROCK, AND SEA SALT)

Chinese cuisine involves a number of thick, tasty sauces or pastes. Most are now easy to find sold in bottles or cans in Chinese markets and some supermarkets. Canned sauces, once opened, should be transferred to screw-top glass jars and kept in the refrigerator where they will last indefinitely.

SAUCES AND PASTES

A bright red, hot sauce which is made from chilies, vinegar, sugar, and salt. It is sometimes used for cooking, but it is most often used in China as a dipping sauce. You should experiment with the various brands available until you find the one you like best. If you find it too strong, dilute it with hot water. Do not confuse this sauce with the chili bean sauce which follows.

CHILI SAUCE

CHILI BEAN SAUCE

This is a thick, dark sauce or paste, hot and spicy, made from yellow soybeans, chilies and other seasonings. Widely used in cooking in western China, there are as many types and varieties as there are people. Be sure to seal the jar tightly after use and store in the refrigerator.

HOISIN SAUCE

Widely used in southern China, this is a thick, dark, brownish red sauce which is made from soybeans, vinegar, sugar, spices and other flavorings. It is sweet and slightly spicy. In the West, it is often used as a sauce for Peking duck instead of the traditional sweet bean sauce. Hoisin sauce is sold in cans and jars and can also be labeled barbecue sauce.

OYSTER SAUCE

A popular seasoning from the fishing villages in southern China, this important sauce is an essential ingredient of Cantonese (southern) cuisine. It is thick and brown and is made from a concentrate of oysters cooked in soy sauce, seasonings and brine. Despite its name, oyster sauce does not taste fishy. It has a rich flavor and is used not only in cooking but as a condiment, diluted with a little oil, for vegetables, poultry, or meats. It is usually sold in bottles and can be bought in Chinese markets and some supermarkets. Search out the most expensive ones; their higher quality is worth the price.

SESAME PASTE

This rich, thick, creamy brown paste is made from toasted sesame seeds, unlike Middle Eastern tahini whose seeds are ground raw. If the paste has separated in the jar, empty the contents into a blender or food processor and blend well. Chinese sesame paste is used in both hot and cold dishes, and is particularly popular in northern and western China. It is sold in jars at Chinese markets. If you can't get it for a recipe, use smooth peanut butter instead.

Used in the south of China, this ingredient adds an exotic flavor and fragrance to dishes. Made from shrimps which are ground and fermented, it has an odor before cooking much stronger than its taste. It is like anchovy paste in texture and can be found in Chinese markets, usually in glass jars. Refrigerated, it will keep indefinitely.

SHRIMP PASTE

Used in northern China as accompaniment to Peking Duck. It is slightly saltier than Hoisin sauce.

SWEET BEAN SAUCE

This thick, spicy, aromatic sauce is made with yellow beans, flour and salt, fermented together. There are two forms: whole beans in a thick sauce; and mashed or puréed beans (sold as crushed bean sauce). I prefer the whole bean variety because it is slightly less salty and has a better texture.

YELLOW BEAN SAUCE/BEAN SAUCE

These are dried seeds of the sesame plant. Unhulled, the seeds range from grayish white to black in color, but once the hull is removed, the sesame seeds are tiny, somewhat flattened, cream colored, and pointed on one end. Sesame seeds are valued throughout Asia, as a flavoring agent and as a source of oil and paste. Keep them in a glass jar in a cool, dry place or keep them frozen. Either way, they will last for weeks.

SESAME SEEDS

Heat a skillet over a burner until hot. Add the sesame seeds and stir occasionally. Watch them closely, and when they begin to lightly brown, about 3 to 5 minutes, stir them again and pour them onto a plate. When they are thoroughly cool, store them in a glass jar in a cool, dark place. Alternatively, you could preheat the oven to No 3/ 325°F/ 170°C. Spread the sesame seeds on a baking sheet. Roast them in the oven for 10 to 15 minutes until they are lightly browned.

TO TOAST SESAME SEEDS

SHALLOTS

Shallots are mild-flavored members of the onion family. They are small, about the size of pickling onions, with copper-red skins. Readily available, they make an excellent substitute for fresh Chinese shallots, which are difficult to find, even in Chinese markets. They are expensive, but their sweet flavor permeates food; a few go a long way. Keep them in a cool, dry place (not the refrigerator).

SHARK'S FIN

Another exotic delicacy of China. Southern Chinese restaurants and expensive restaurants in other areas of China sometimes offer a long list of shark's fin dishes. Extremely expensive, this is a conspicuous symbol of extravagance. The fin means the dorsal "comb fin" or the two ventral fins of any of a variety of sharks; indeed, in China, fins are imported from all over the world. Preparation usually involves an elaborate process of soaking and boiling in several changes of water and stocks. However, thanks to modern technology, you can now purchase prepared shark's fin in the freezer section of the Chinese market.

Like bird's nest, another highly sought after Chinese delicacy, it has little flavor but is prized for its clear, gelatinous strands and texture. It is usually served with a rich stock, or stuffed in poultry or scrambled with eggs and crab.

SICHUAN PEPPERCORNS

Sichuan peppercorns are known through China as "flower peppers" because they look like flower buds opening. They are reddish-brown in color with a strong, pungent odor which distinguishes them from the hotter black peppercorns. They are actually not a pepper at all, but are the dried berries of a shrub which is a member of the citrus family. Their smell reminds me of lavender, while their taste is sharp, numbing and mildly spicy. They can be ground in a conventional pepper mill but should be roasted (see below) before they are ground to bring out their full flavor. An expensive item, they are sold wrapped in cellophane or plastic bags in Chinese stores. They will keep indefinitely if stored in a well sealed container.

TO ROAST SICHUAN PEPPERCORNS

Heat a wok or frying pan over a medium heat. Add the peppercorns (up to ¼ cup at a time) and stir-fry them for about 5 minutes until they brown slightly and start to smoke. Remove the pan from the heat and let them cool. Grind the peppercorns in a peppermill, clean coffee grinder, or with a mortar and pestle. Seal the mixture tightly in a screw-top jar to store. Alternatively, keep the whole roasted peppercorns in a well-sealed container and grind them when required.

SICHUAN PRESERVED VEGETABLE

There are many types of Chinese pickled vegetables. One of the most popular is Sichuan preserved vegetable, a speciality of Sichuan Province. This is the root of the mustard green, pickled in salt and hot chilies. It is sold in cans in Chinese grocery stores and gives a pleasantly crunchy texture and spicy taste to dishes. Before using it, rinse in cold water and then slice or chop as required. Any unused vegetable should be transferred to a tightly covered jar and stored in the refrigerator where it will keep indefinitely.

SILK SQUASH – CHINESE OKRA

A popular vegetable frequently found in markets in China, this is a long, thin, cylindrical squash, tapering at one end with deep, narrow ridges. Choose firm, unblemished dark green ones. Peel away the ridges. If the vegetable is young, you can leave on some of the green; if older, it's best to peel away all the skin. The inside flesh turns soft, spongy and tender as it cooks, tasting like a cross between a cucumber and courgette. Absorbent, it readily picks up flavors of the sauce or food it is cooked with.

SNOW PEAS/ MANGETOUT BEANS

Smaller varieties of snow peas are found in the markets of China; the larger ones are found in the

West. But all of them are sweet and crispy. In China, snow peas are simply stir-fried, with a little oil and salt, and bits of garlic and ginger root. Often they are combined with meats. Look for pods that are firm with very small peas, which means they are tender and young.

SOY SAUCES

Soy sauce is an essential ingredient in China's cooking. It is made from a mixture of soybeans, flour and water, which is then naturally fermented and aged for some months. The distilled liquid is soy sauce. There are two main types:

LIGHT SOY SAUCE

As the name implies, this is light in color, but it is full of flavor and is the best one to use for cooking. It is known in Chinese markets as Superior Soy and is saltier than dark soy sauce.

DARK SOY SAUCE

This sauce is aged for much longer than light soy sauce, hence its darker, almost black color. It is slightly thicker and stronger than light soy sauce and is more suitable for stews. I prefer it to light soy as a dipping sauce. It is known in Chinese markets as Soy Superior Sauce, and, although used less often than light soy, it is important to have some at hand.

SPINACH

The Western varieties of spinach are quite different from those used in China, nevertheless they make satisfactory substitutes for the Chinese variety. Spinach is most commonly stir-fried, so frozen spinach is obviously unsuitable. Chinese water spinach is what's most frequently cooked in China and is available in Chinese markets in the West. It has hollow stems and delicate, green, pointed leaves, lighter in color than common spinach and with a milder taste. It should be cooked when it is very fresh, preferably on the day on which it is bought.

STAR ANISE

Star anise is the hard, star-shaped seed-pod of he anise bush. (It is also known as Chinese anise or whole anise.) It is similar in flavor and fragrance to common anise seed but is more robust and liquorice-like. Star anise is an essential ingredient of five-spice powder and is widely used in braised dishes to impart a rich taste and fragrance. Sold by Chinese markets in plastic packs, it should be stored in a tightly covered jar in a cool, dry place.

SUGAR

Sugar has been used – sparingly – in the cooking of savory dishes in China for a thousand years. Excessive sugar destroys the palate, but when properly employed, it helps balance the various flavors of sauces and other dishes. Chinese sugar comes in several forms: as rock or yellow lump sugar, as brown sugar slabs, and as maltose or malt sugar. I particularly like to use rock sugar which is richer and has a more subtle flavor than that of refined, granulated sugar. It also gives a good luster and glaze to braised dishes and sauces. Buy it in Chinese markets, where it is usually sold in packages. You may need to break the lumps into smaller pieces with a wooden mallet or rolling pin. If you cannot find it, you can use white sugar or raw sugar (the amber, chunky kind) instead.

VINEGAR

Vinegars are widely used in China as dipping sauces as well as for cooking. Unlike Western vinegars, they are usually made from rice. There are many varieties, ranging in flavor from the spicy and slightly tart to the sweet and pungent:

WHITE RICE VINEGAR

Clear and mild in flavor. It has a faint taste of glutinous rice and is used for sweet and sour dishes.

BLACK RICE VINEGAR

Very dark in color with a rich but mild taste. It is used for braised dishes, noodles, and sauces.

RED RICE VINEGAR   Sweet and spicy in taste, it is usually used as a
dipping sauce for seafood.

All these vinegars can be bought in Chinese
markets and will keep indefinitely. If you cannot
get Chinese vinegars, I suggest you use cider vinegar instead. Malt vinegar and wine vinegars cannot be substituted because their taste is too strong.

WATER CHESTNUTS   Water chestnuts do not actually belong to the
chestnut family at all, but are a sweet, white and
crunchy root vegetable about the size of a wal-
nut. They are especially popular in the south,
where they are sometimes grown between rice
plants in paddies. (This is why the fresh ones are
often muddy on the outside. They must be peeled
before eating or cooking.) Sweet, crisp water chestnuts have been eaten in China for centuries, where
they are eaten as a snack, having first been boiled
in their skins, or peeled and simmered in rock
sugar. They are also used in many cooked dishes.

Here, fresh and canned water chestnuts can be
obtained from Chinese markets or some supermarkets. When buying fresh ones, look for a firm,
hard texture. The skin should be tight and taut, not
wrinkled. If they are mushy, they are too old. Feel
them all over for soft, rotten spots. If you peel
them in advance, cover them with cold water to
prevent browning and store them in the refrigerator. They will keep, unpeeled, in a paper bag in
the refrigerator for up to two weeks.

Canned water chestnuts are a pale version of the
fresh ones, with a good texture but little taste
because both the crispness and the flavor are lost
in the canning process. Rinse them well in cold
water before you use them, and store any unused
ones in a jar of cold water. They will keep for several weeks in the refrigerator if you change the
water daily. Fresh jicama, a crisp tuber, is a suitable substitute for water chestnuts and is prefer-
able to the canned.

WHEAT GLUTEN

This is made from washing out the starch from wheat dough until only the adhesive substance remains. Once it is made, it can be boiled or deep-fried, then cooked with other ingredients. It is a staple and mock meat for Chinese vegetarians.

WHEAT STARCH

Wheat starch is a flour-like powder left after the protein is removed from the wheat flour. It is used as a wrapping for dumplings in China. Bought in Chinese markets, it will keep indefinitely tightly sealed and kept in a cool, dry place.

WONTON/HUNTUN SKINS

Wonton skins are made from egg and flour and can be bought fresh or frozen from Chinese markets. They are thin pastry-like wrappings, stretched like freshly-made noodles, which can be stuffed with minced meat and fried, steamed, or used in soups. They are sold in little piles of 3 in/ 7.5 cm squares, sometimes a bit larger, wrapped in plastic. The number of squares or skins in a package varies from about 30 to 36, depending upon the supplier. Fresh wonton skins will keep for about five days if stored in plastic wrap or a plastic bag in the refrigerator. If you are using frozen wonton skins, just peel off the number you require and thaw them thoroughly before you use them.

YUNNAN AND JINHUA HAM

China produces some of the best hams in the world. In China you will see preserved whole Yunnan and Jinhua (from Zhejiang province) hams hanging in food shops, but the ham is also available in cans. Unfortunately, it is not obtainable in the West. I find Italian prosciutto and American Smithfield hams acceptable substitutes for the wonderfully rich, smoky-flavored Chinese hams.

INDEX TO THE RECIPES